REBIRTH

REBIRTH

OUTLIVING THE SOVIET GRIP ON BOTH SIDES OF THE ATLANTIC

INGRID POPA FOTINO

DEDICATION

To the memory of Sandu and Liliana Economu, their parents,
and all those who were executed in Yugoslavia
under the Soviet impetus, 1948–1950

ACKNOWLEDGMENTS

I began work on my memoir more than thirty years ago, when my friend Susan Boulding offered to take my daughters to her house, freeing me to write. On the road to Flagstaff Mountain, I spotted a parking space with a panoramic view of Boulder. There, in the car, I started jotting down a few snippets of reminiscences from my childhood, doubting I would remember much. But as I did so, images and impressions started to flood my consciousness.

Susan was the first of a long series of family, friends, and colleagues who extended their helping hands along the path to writing my memoir and to healing. In particular, Shelby Frisch, my neighbor, office mate, and friend, listened with interest to my endeavor and suggested I start jotting down just one recollection, any one, and take it from there—to approach my task from the lighter side, or to write as if I looked at myself from the outside, from far away, to ward off the pain. His constant support and gentle understanding were most helpful at a time when I felt very vulnerable.

The writers' group in Boulder, Colorado, started by Ann Scarboro when our children were little, included Susan Boucher and Silvia Pettem, who encouraged my writing by sharing caring insights.

Summit Middle School Principal David Finell offered his empathy and support and, together with the parents of the Summit Board, allowed me the scheduling flexibility I needed to write my memoir.

Every year while I taught at Summit, the teachers of World Geography and International Relations invited me into their classes to share my childhood experiences with their students. Chris Koch, the first of these supportive educators, guided me in presenting the positive aspects of my story. Alex Garcia, who took over after Chris left, showed me how to present what I wanted to say in a format that would be relevant to the material the students were studying. Cheryle Kapsak, the Ancient World History teacher, attempted to expose her sixth graders, in as gentle a way as possible, to my rough contact with the world as a child. Cheryle, together with my friend Kendra Bartley, the school counselor, encouraged me in my writing. These Summit friends and colleagues all contributed to my recovery and my Colorado roots.

Sebastian Doreanu offered me access to the library of meaningful books he has been collecting, including the biography of Father Leu and Slawomir Rawicz's *The Long Walk*. In general, these historical resources were most helpful.

Cathy and Wayne Grider read the first chapters of my memoir and made me feel they presented some interest; in addition, Cathy provided valuable editing suggestions.

My husband encouraged my effort from the very beginning, offered feedback on the material with which he was familiar, and provided some very meticulous editing. I am deeply thankful to him.

My elder daughter, Domnica, was my first "biographer" when, in about third grade, she started writing "Mommy's story," slowly, laboriously, asking for the spelling of words, until my discomfort and restlessness discouraged her and she gave up. She resumed her input after I wrote "my story" myself many years later and contributed her comments on the chapters relating to our experience as a family.

My younger daughter, Adriana, read and tirelessly edited my entire, unabridged draft, sharing and discussing her sharp and constructive insights. She was really my first editor, and her interest and contributions were most meaningful and enriching to me.

Both daughters joined forces and split the work for one last review of the entire book before it went to print. I cannot overemphasize how moved I am by their generous encouragement, support, and care.

My friend and principal editor, Sandra Rush, who gave shape and flow to the final version of the book, guided me, encouraged me, and sustained me throughout, even allowing me to push beyond the norm. She brought to the editing task not only her expertise, but also her heart. I feel we shared a precious experience together.

I am deeply thankful to Jan Stansen, whose family adopted us as soon as we arrived in Colorado. She offered her enthusiasm and spontaneous generosity by applying her professional skills to the design of the cover of this book.

I was soothed and emboldened by all the friends and acquaintances—too many to name individually here—at work, at school, at church, even strangers, who listened with compassion, some with moving understanding.

I extend my deepest gratitude to all.

Boulder, October 26, 2018

TABLE OF CONTENTS

AUTHOR'S NOTE

At a time when Vladimir Putin considers the demise of the Soviet Union as "the greatest geopolitical catastrophe of the century,"[†] and when he seems to be aiming for its revival, my goal in writing this memoir is to impart a feeling for the impact of the Soviet Union in the countries it subjugated and particularly for the terrifying application of Lenin's teachings. I also strive to expose the extent of the grip of the Soviet Union into Western Europe, especially into French culture and education, and even across the Atlantic into the United States and its media, its academia, its government.

Simultaneously with Putin's desire to resurrect at least some aspects of the Soviet Union, the past Soviet impact is whitewashed, and new generations are unaware of it. Ana Blandiana, one of the most highly acclaimed contemporary Romanian poets and dissidents, founder of the Memorial to the Victims of Communism and to the Resistance, and recipient of the US State Department's *Romanian Women of Courage Award* (2014), expresses this phenomenon: "The greatest victory of communism, a victory dramatically revealed only after 1989, was to create people without a memory—a brainwashed new man unable to remember what he was, what he had, or what he did before communism. The creation of the Memorial of the Victims of Communism and

[†]Associated Press, updated April 25, 2005, 2:30:13 p.m. ET.

of the Resistance is a means of counteracting this victory, a means to resuscitate the collective memory." I aim to contribute to this resuscitation.

Finally, I would like to share the effects of the stunning events of 1989 and the exuberant fireworks they launched: the fall of the Berlin wall, the demise of one communist regime after another in the Soviet sphere, the melting of the Iron Curtain, and even, two years later, the collapse of the Soviet Union. All borders were opened, allowing us to reunite with family and friends after more than four decades of almost total separation and to reconnect with our country of origin. A burst of hope was suddenly released, a sense that rebuilding and recovery were possible, producing the eerie feeling that there is life after death, or, even more, that we were headed toward rebirth.

1
THE RETURN

As we contemplated the unimaginable—a return trip to the land from which we had escaped 43 years earlier, all bridges cut—my fears were echoed by exiled Romanian writer Vintilă Horia as he himself mulled over a possible return to our homeland.

> *It is such an overwhelming event in my life, just the thought, just the word "return" home, that I wonder every day and every night, since I cannot sleep because of this, how I will react when I step off the plane . . . will I faint, will I die, will I cry, will I drop down to kiss the ground. . . . It's one of the great questions that still hover over my future.*[1]

---

[1]The original Romanian text: "*E un lucru aşa de covârşitor în existenţa mea, numai ideea, numai cuvântul întoarcere acasă, încât îmi pun problema în fiecare zi şi în fiecare noapte, pentru că nu pot să dorm din cauza asta, cum o să reacţionez când o să mă dau jos din avion . . . o să leşin, o să mor, o să plâng, o să cad jos ca să sărut pământul...e una din întrebările mari care plutesc încă în viitorul meu.*"

The author, Vintilă Horia, was the 1960 recipient of the Goncourt Prize, the prestigious French literature award for the best novel of the year. See his interview by journalist Marilena Rotaru in "*Intoarcerea lui Vintilă Horia*," ("The Return of Vintilă Horia," Ed. *Ideea*, Bucharest, 2002, p. 11).

I did not faint. I did not cry. But the return to my native Romania shook me to the core. For more than a year since the possibility of the inconceivable began to take shape, ocean waves had pummeled me at night in my sleep. The inner turmoil was pervasive.

Ever since my 18th birthday, I understood the futility of my preparations to be ready to help rebuild my country of birth after the Soviet devastation: the repressive Communist regime imposed by the Soviet troops in 1946 was there to stay. Just as the Soviet colossus crushed the Hungarian Revolution in 1956, just as Soviet tanks rolled into Czechoslovakia in 1968, just as they threatened Poland into submission, the Soviets would again overpower any move toward liberation.

For the next several decades, I devoted every ounce of energy to pluck out of the deepest folds of my being the hope of ever returning to Romania, the world I suddenly lost at age eight. To move ahead with my life, I had to give up the world that had given me a family, a language, a culture, an identity.

After decades of striving with all my might to accept the fact that I could never set foot again on Romanian soil nor see the family and friends we left there, suddenly, in the fall of 1989, European events exploded. The Berlin wall was hammered down on November 9, and the Iron Curtain[2] was pierced in Germany, in Hungary, in Poland, in Czechoslovakia . . . and eventually in Romania. The unfathomable had happened: we could return!

Excitement and hopeful expectation mingled with anxiety: the desolation in East Berlin after decades of Soviet occupation, the shootings in Bucharest when Ceaușescu[3] fell, the persistent remnants

---

[2]A term coined by Winston Churchill on March 5, 1946, at Westminster College in Fulton, Missouri. It referred to the separation between the Communist European countries and the rest of the Western world. See Appendix B.

[3]General Secretary of the Romanian Communist Party (1965–1989) and head of the state until his execution on December 25, 1989.

of the secret police. The ghosts of the past were even more frightening than the reality of the present.

As soon as Ceauşescu was executed on December 25, 1989, I called my Uncle Horia in Bucharest. I heard his warm, welcoming voice for the first time since I was eight—a span of 41 years. He advised me: "Wait until the situation settles somewhat and then you can safely come."

After a year of anticipation, it was time for decisions. Do I go with my husband alone or do we take our daughters? How would this trip affect them? I needed my husband's and my children's support to come face-to-face with my immense childhood loss and my trepidation about the reality awaiting us.

The apprehension of my return came in spasms. My American friend Marion Paton shared her own life experience in pointing the way out: "You will not go back, you will not return to the Romania you left. You will go forward to the Romania of the future, to Romania as it is being transformed, to its recovery." A recovery to which we could, hopefully, contribute.

Suddenly, the waves subsided and the decision was made: my husband Mircea and I would travel to Romania with our two daughters: "You do not want to exclude them from an experience that may be life-changing" advised our friends. Each daughter came to terms with her own quandary: 19-year-old Domnica, a college student at the time, worried about the extra expense, and 14-year old Adriana was concerned about missing out on the enchantingly festive 4th of July in Chautauqua Park in Boulder, where we lived, perhaps our last as we had considered a move to another state. They both decided to accompany us.

On June 20, 1991, we were on our way. The flight to Paris was uneventful, but panic struck me at Orly Airport when, after a couple of days' visit, our friend Jean Odiot dropped us off for the flight to Bucharest. As we watched him wave goodbye, I saw my life in the Free

World drift away and my haunting fears take over: "Our last link to the Western world. Our last link to freedom. Our last link . . ."

What had I done? Why was I returning when my parents had risked so much to get us out? In my mind's eye, I saw the wrenching escape, the courage to go through with it, the killings, the luck it took us to reach the West; I saw the uninterrupted chain of supportive hands stretching from Boulder to New York to Paris toward my husband's and my native land. All the warmth, generosity, and sharing we experienced over almost a lifetime What if I am never able to come back? Why was I giving it all up?

Nonsense, of course. There was no reason we would not return to our solidly established home in the West. But panic is resonance with past wounds and fears. It is not rational.

Heading to the check-in counter, I eyed with apprehension the weighing of our suitcases. Would they be overweight? Would we have to pay a surcharge when our finances were so precarious? Would the staff of TAROM,[4] the Romanian government airline, unused to the courtesies required by a free market, be petty and unpleasant at a time when I felt so vulnerable?

The passengers preparing to board with us were a disquieting bunch, quite different from the ones we had normally encountered in our travels. A feeling of far away, unfamiliar populations—nothing reminiscent of the "melting pot" of the United States. And not many Romanian-looking passengers.

The lady at the counter for Air France, which partnered with TAROM, greeted us with a smile. My panic started to subside. It's human cruelty that scares and hurts, not practical obstacles.

The flight was close to regular standards, except for the expected soiled, paperless toilets. Inside the aircraft, signs in Romanian everywhere awed me. "Look, girls! Did you see *this*? And *that*?" I

---

[4]TAROM is the acronym for **T**ransporturile **A**eriene **ROM**âne.

would point over and over to Romanian words, the first I had seen in public display for almost half a century.

The food on the plane was dubious. The bread had a rancid smell and we left it uneaten. The meat didn't seem to be fresh, but it was all right. I concentrated on the view below us. A French lady had generously relinquished her seat by the window so Mircea could sit next to me, Domnica sat in the row behind us, and Adriana sat behind her.

"You will see a sudden change as you fly over Romania," my mother had predicted, vicariously experiencing this return through us. "You will see the Mureş River and the Olt, and the whole landscape will suddenly turn colorful and varied. There will be large forests and many, many rivers."

Our Romanian friends in Denver had laughed, "You will see nothing! It will all be covered by clouds."

There were clouds indeed, scattered flocks of white opaqueness interspersed with clear openings. There were expanses of plains, a brownish color with a large body of water. Lake Balaton in Hungary, we surmised. Then patches of different colors appeared, yellow and green and orange, then dark green on what looked like hills and valleys, and shiny streams lacing the green.

"This is Romania," said the man behind us who, like the other passengers, had noted our restless curiosity and excitement as we communicated across our three rows. "We are flying over Transylvania," he added. He had attended an air conference in Paris and was, I believe, a pilot. Nice. Friendly. Subdued, as a man who had endured enough in life not to expend energy in excitement or needless expressions of emotion. All the population in Romania was to share that fatigue.

The mountains were to the left of us, and the man pointed to Bucharest. The plane dropped in altitude as we approached Otopeni

Airport for our landing. I was mesmerized by the spot where we would touch down.

"Home. I am back home. This is the longest trip I have ever taken. Forty-three years," I explained to our fellow passenger. He smiled. "Welcome to Romania."

2

END OF WORLD WAR II: THE SOVIET CLAMPDOWN 1944–1947

Romania . . .

A sunny land, a loving, all-understanding mother, and a stranger who dared kiss her: my father. Dreams filled with visions of falling airplanes; air raids that sent us cramming under the stairwell—these were war times; the ominous rumble of the monstrous landslide that was to obliterate our world and sear our lives over several generations.

Romania, at the beginning of World War II, was threatened with territorial dismemberment on two fronts: If the Axis won the war, Romania would lose a large part of Transylvania. If the Allies won the war, it would lose the province of Bessarabia. In June 1940, as the Germans were pursuing their blitzkrieg in Western Europe, the Soviet forces took over Bessarabia. In June of the following year, when Hitler invaded the Soviet Union, Romanian General Ion Antonescu, having now assumed dictatorial powers, joined him in order to recover the lost province and stop the advance of the Soviet troops. This, unfortunately, meant eventual war against all the Allies, including England and the United States, with whom the overwhelming majority of Romanians sympathized and whom they never regarded as enemies.*

***Romania 1866–1947*, Keith Hitchins, Clarendon Press, Oxford, 1944, pp. 471 and 489.

War Rumbles in My Childhood Paradise

After Romanian and German troops retrieved Bessarabia, the continued advance of the troops into Soviet territory became very unpopular in Romania. The imminent defeat of the Axis after Stalingrad (February 1943) made Romania's pursuit of an armistice ever more pressing. The hope was to deal with the British and American governments with the aim of avoiding a Soviet occupation and reinstating a democratic government in Romania. As Prime Minister Antonescu could not be persuaded to consider an armistice, 22-year-old King Michael, together with the leaders of the traditional parties, removed him from power in the coup of August 23, 1944. Great Britain and the United States had already been approached to discuss the terms of the armistice, on the model of the one negotiated by the Italians the previous year. The British and US governments, however, insisted that Romania deal with the Soviet Union. The armistice Romania was practically obliged to sign stipulated, among other conditions, the unhindered movement of Soviet troops on Romanian territory. Soviet troops started pouring into Romania even before the September 12, 1944, signing of the armistice agreement and occupied most of the country as enemy territory.* The Soviet Union annexed Bessarabia and renamed it "the Republic of Moldova," even though "Moldova" was the name of another existing province of Romania.

**Romania 1866–1947*, Keith Hitchins, Clarendon Press, Oxford, 1944, p. 496.

"Come, come see the airplanes!" my father beckoned excitedly when the sirens sent people rushing to an underground shelter dug near the hamlet of Domneşti, north of Bucharest, where we had taken refuge. He took me with him to the open field.

"Ervin, bring the child back!!" My mother's frantic calls were met with his boyish smile and the reminder: "Soviet planes never hit on target."

(US planes, however, did, as I heard repeatedly as an adult. On April 4, 1944, the sirens brought the curious—but not my father—to the city's rooftops. This time, the planes were American, aiming for the railway station. Thousands of civilians died in Bucharest that day.)

When the bombings ended, both Soviet and American, the Soviet troops arrived atop heavy tanks, led by what seemed to me to be fat, ugly men in drab uniforms speaking a repulsive language I could not understand. Why were they filling our streets? Why did they force Aunt Marcella to leave her home?

"Aunt" Marcella Cezianu, an elderly family friend, lived in a cheerful house shaded by a huge chestnut tree. I was four years old when I would cross, alone, the street that separated her house from ours, unaware of my mother's watchful eye by the window nor of the policeman at the corner of the street. I would enter the sun-spotted courtyard, step by the maze of fallen chestnuts, and climb the spiral stairs to her apartment. Aunt Marcella would open the door, sit me at a little round table, and start building castles by balancing playing cards on top of each other. Or she would give me decals to hold against the window and moisten with water until they sprang into sudden shape and color. It was a world of magic that filled me with joy and wonder, a world to which I could walk all by myself.

A world that crumbled one afternoon when the door opened on an arresting sight: Aunt Marcella was slumped on the couch, in tears, surrounded by friends: "they" had come and ordered her to leave.

Gloom and silence permeated the room. Occasionally her soft cry would reach my ears: "What shall I do? Where shall I go?"

Her distress filled me with anxiety. Still, I was too young to suspect that our turn would come next, just before the birth of my sister, for whose arrival I had prayed every evening and for whom I had already knit one woolen slipper.

* * *

As I learned later, Soviet soldiers were seen scrutinizing our apartment building shortly before my sister was born. My father was warned of this. That very night he took out as many of our belongings as he could. The next day the Soviet soldiers arrived and ordered us to move out within 24 hours. They inspected our lodging and indicated which of our belongings we could take with us and which were to be left behind.

"What's that?" They pointed to the small refrigerator that my mother, in anticipation of the question, had filled with my clothes.

"It's a child's hamper."

"Take it, we don't need it."

Such incidents would feed the countless jokes about Soviet soldiers and their unfamiliarity with modern amenities. They were seen wearing several watches on their arms and Soviet women wore bras over their clothes as decorations.

To her enormous relief, my mother was also allowed to take the piano, a most precious heirloom that had belonged to my grandmother, who died when my mother was only five. With these treasures, without blankets (the Soviets needed them) but with bed linen (they had no use for that), we moved into the apartment of my Uncle Arnold, who was away on the Front. The apartment was in a tall, 12-story edifice, "blocul Wilson," named after the US president.

The Soviet occupation forces had imposed a curfew: anyone who was in the streets after dark would be shot, including doctors on emergency calls. Inevitably, as evening approached, my mother felt contraction pains. She rushed to the doctor, who gave her a shot to delay labor. In the morning, no sign of impending labor. This procedure was repeated for several anxious weeks. Finally, my sister's birth was induced, in the morning.

At age five with my baby sister, in 1945.

* * *

When my Uncle Arnold returned from the Front, the Soviet troops were now a constant, ominous presence in our city. We moved into a.

house of our own that had been damaged during the war and was being repaired, on Strada Paris.

How can it be that some of my life's happiest, sunniest recollections are tied to that house? I can still see it—an aesthetic three-story structure with peach-colored stucco walls, the bright sun rays bouncing off the white steps leading to the main entrance; the slender cherry tree that yielded its first fruit in time for my May birthday; the huge linden tree on the sidewalk by the gate with a canopy of flowers that filled the evening air with a sweet, intoxicating aroma.

> "Lili Marlen" was a World War II love song interpreted by renowned anti-Nazi singer Marlene Dietrich. It was a favorite with the Allied troops but resented by the Soviets as an expression of the Western powers, whose influence they strived to eliminate. The end of the war had brought tension between the Soviet Union and their Western Allies over control of the occupied territories and competition between opposing political systems.

Inside, the vast, luminous living room housed my mother's precious piano on which rested a hand-wound record player. I would strain to hear my favorite song, "Lili Marlen," which we could play, but only with the volume turned down. The Soviets had taken over the house next door, and it was risky to have them hear it, because the song was very popular with the Western Allies. A wide stairway led to the second floor where my little sister and I had a room to ourselves.

To celebrate my sixth birthday, in 1946, my mother invited several friends to a costume party, a very special event in a culture unfamiliar with Halloween. My father appeared just long enough to kiss me and wish me "*La mulţi ani!*"—a traditional Romanian birthday wish meaning "May you live many years."

My father had no longer time to spare. No more joyous rides on his shoulders, no more late evening kisses when he returned from work. I was too young to suspect that he was deeply preoccupied by the changes that were being forced on our country by the Soviets' presence, threatening life as we knew it in general and private enterprise in

My mini-world on the large stairway of our house on Strada Paris (from top): my best friends Anca and Tudor with their mother Janine, my sister in our mother's arms next to me, Aunt Nana holding my cousins Rucky and Mihai, Aunt Mioara with my cousin Andy.

particular—threatening even our freedom, for my father had already been arrested once.[5]

As CEO of the cotton and jute mill Dobrogeana, my father had been summoned by the newly installed Attorney General to provide some information. Dobrogeana was built in 1937 in the Black Sea port of Constanţa by my father and his father to meet the growing demand for sacks required to transport goods. My father bought state-of-the-art machinery and electric motors from Scotland as well as from Siemens in Berlin, reputedly the biggest producer of electric motors at that time. Eventually, he oversaw the management of two other textile enterprises,

[5]More than 40 years later, I asked my father about his arrest. The information about his arrest is from my taped conversation with him in 1988.

Năvodul and Industria Bumbacului, employing 6,000 workers altogether in three shifts, day and night, to support the war effort. These achievements were being threatened by the Soviet-imposed Communist regime.

My father went to the Court House, and the Attorney General gave orders not to let him go. Fortunately, the brother-in-law of one of my grandfather's associates happened to be at the Court House at the same time and noticed that my father was being led away by a guard. He came close to my father, who managed to say only: "They have arrested me." The brother-in-law immediately called my grandfather. Meanwhile, my father was led downstairs, fingerprinted, and brought back upstairs for his arrest to be confirmed. But my grandfather was already there with a lawyer, and he managed to have my father released on bond.

My Grandfather

My grandfather, Apostol Popa, had a monumental influence in my life. His joy in me, his first grandchild, seemed boundless. Nothing in the world would distract his attention when he was playing with me, not even my grandmother's announcement that moths had eaten into some prized oriental rug: "Did you hear what I said?" she insisted. His reported reply was simply "I'm busy now, I am playing with my granddaughter."

My grandfather would take me on his fishing trips and teach me how to hook the bait. He could look at a basket of apples and, without cutting any of them open, know exactly which ones contained worms. With his slow gait he walked with me through my Uncle Valter's orchard in Constanţa, pointing out the different types of trees, picking up caterpillars with his fingers and sharing with me his intimate familiarity with nature. He initiated me, as well, to the steps of Viennese waltzes and to the rules of backgammon.

My grandfather holding me on his shoulders; my head is seen between my parents' heads; my grandmother is on the extreme left, next to my mother's sister Lydia; my father's sister Helga is on the extreme right, next to her husband Horia.

Once he commented with satisfaction: "You are worth a boy and a half!" "A *boy* and a half?" I puzzled inwardly. "Why not a *girl* and a half?" But mathematics weighed more heavily than gender and I felt very pleased indeed.

My grandfather could have been the subject of an American success story: One of seven children, he lost his father as a boy and dropped out of school when he turned 14 to help his family earn a living. Starting with a job at Pantazi's fabric store, he moved on to the customs department of Schenker, a well-known international transportation company headquartered in Vienna.

At Schenker, building in time on his skill and tenacity, my grandfather was entrusted with ever greater responsibilities. Especially lucrative was his idea to transport European coal on the Danube, from the port of Galaţi in Romania to the port of Răduevăţ in Yugoslavia. There the coal was delivered to the Bor copper mines and copper ore was brought back. As a result of this and other initiatives, my grandfather was compensated with one-third of the earnings of Schenker's Romanian branch. Eventually, he became the head of the Romanian branch of the company, with headquarters in Bucharest and offices in Galaţi, Constanţa, and Cernăuţi.

My grandfather was elected six times to Romania's Senate and fought, in a world dominated by multinational companies, for the interests of his young country. From it all he emerged patient and relaxed, a contented family man at peace with himself and with the world.

At least with the world we knew then. How did he fare once that world was totally upended by the Soviet occupation and the dictatorial regime it imposed, when all his possessions were taken away? How did he fare when his son-in-law spent more than 16 years in prison and his daughter, as the wife of a political prisoner, could not be hired by the government, the only employer in the Communist system? She had to hide the fact that her husband was incarcerated, while her young sons were often taunted by their teachers: "How come your father doesn't visit you? How come your father does not send a birthday gift? How come your father . . . ?"

What happened to my grandfather's serenity when my father, his first-born, attempted to escape with his young family and he did not know where they were or if they had made it? Was he able to find peace in that world? I never had a chance to ask him. The last echoes we heard of him were toward the end of his life, when he had lost part of his memory and he would repeatedly leave the house with a suitcase in his hand saying, when asked where he was going, that he was going to see his son (my father).

By the time I turned nine, we had left Romania, and I never saw or talked with him again. But by then, he had branded me as surely as if he had guided my steps throughout life.

The Lights of My Childhood: Tudor, Anca, and Lessons with Mrs. Livianu

Giving in to my intense yearning to identify the letters of the alphabet, my parents hired a private teacher, Mrs. Livianu, to cover the first-grade curriculum with me because students could not be enrolled in school before the age of seven and I was only six.

Mrs. Livianu was very strict—we were to concentrate on studying and nothing else. But then what worlds of boundless wonder she unfolded before my enchanted eyes! She spoke of animals and insects and trees and plants, of wondrous lands where people did not speak Romanian and one in particular in which lakes were so close to mountains that, within the very same day, you could ski in the morning and bathe in the afternoon: Switzerland!

I learned to decipher words and, best of all, to unravel the mysteries of arithmetic. Division seemed nothing short of miraculous and held for me a fascination I can still sense to this day. With the confidence imparted by the mastery of division, I progressed to dreams of science and the exploration of the changes occurring in nature, for with the passing months I realized that magic belonged to tales, not to the real world. The universe and its mysteries seemed well within reach. (I did not know then that we are not ruled by the light of our mind alone, as I so proudly believed, but also by the blind persistence of past wounds and trauma.)

Since I was home-schooled, my life was very lonely, spent mainly with mother and Tereza, the cook, and longing for my weekly meetings with my best friends Tudor and Anca, who were the lights of my childhood.

One year older than I was, Anca was always cheerful and ready to play. I envied her intensely black hair, shining so it looked almost blue, a color my light brown braids in no way approached. Tudor was two and a half years older than I. His knowledge much surpassed Anca's and mine; his gift for drawing prompted admiring comments from the adults and his playful, mocking laughter and boyish self-assurance never ceased to move me.

Yet, despite the age difference, I could hold my own with them—or they allowed me to—as when we played "war": hiding behind pillows with the lights out, we each held the flag of a country of our choice and strove to grab the others' flags in the total obscurity of the living room. There were no real enemies, for none of us wanted to be the Soviet Union. Tudor was England, where he was born; Anca was France, an all-time favorite and the residence of her great-uncle; and I was Romania, with an ardor that almost made me win when, suddenly, a piercing scream brought our contest to a screeching halt: a pair of scrawny legs were caught in the frenzy of our play, and they belonged, alas, to my friends' grandmother. She had strayed, unguardedly, into the darkness of the room and, in shock, displayed an utter lack of sympathy for our enthusiastic clashes. We had to stop.

Last Chance to Leave Romania: To Return or Not to Return?

The year was 1947. Our family was leaving Bucharest for a trip to Switzerland and Italy. This was indeed an incredible occurrence since, after the war ended, the Soviet troops occupied Romania, cutting us off from the free part of the world. Special permission was required to leave the country, and it was practically never granted to families, out of concern that if no family member was left behind, the government had no leverage to ensure the family would return. My father, nevertheless, had obtained permission to go on a business trip with us.

Italy shines through, as I recall that trip, for no other country quite gripped my heart as it did, despite a language I could not understand. "*Como ti chiami?*" ("What's your name?"), a friendly voice would ask me. To my inquiring look, my mother would point out the similarity to the Romanian "*Cum te chiamă?*" but I did not grasp it. However, the faces that asked my name were so smiling, so inviting, how could I misunderstand the warmth they exuded?

I thrived on the views of the Lago Maggiore and its enchanted islands; on the spectacular apparition of the Duomo cathedral in Milan, all sculptured lacework reaching for the sky; on the chocolate-covered, heart-shaped "gelato"; on the visit to the Pitti Palace in Florence, the one museum I thoroughly enjoyed as a child. And everywhere, the Italians' glowing enthusiasm for life in general and for my little sister in particular: "*Che bella! Che carina!*" ("How beautiful! How lovely!"). What was so great about a two-year-old? I was seven and I knew so much more than she did. "Someday," I consoled myself, "she will also be seven."

After a few weeks though, much as I loved Italy, I started longing for Romania. I wanted to be in my room again, to see my friends, my grandparents, to speak Romanian. I wanted home!

The return trip was bathed in sadness. The restaurants in Vienna were depleted, Budapest was dark and crumbling, the people in the streets seemed hungry—not for food, but for something I did not know. The contrast was, for me, incomprehensible. Why were Austria and Hungary so different from Italy?[6]

---

[6] That trip revealed the stark contrast between Italy and the countries to the east of it. They had all lost the war, but the Allied troops had withdrawn from Italy, whereas Austria (its eastern part), Hungary, and Romania remained now under Soviet control. It also made me sense the Romanians' inherent affinity for the Italians.

The real shock came, however, when we returned to Romania. I had waited, longed to be back, yet my homeland appeared like a low, oppressive cover of uninterrupted gray clouds, and a people subdued by infinite sadness. I could not believe that everyone spoke Romanian, even waiters in restaurants, yet there was no joy in that because they all looked burdened. There was a pervasive feeling of such sorrow that even now, many decades later, I can only cry inwardly at the recollection. There was no laughter, no gleam in people's eyes, none of the Italians' mirth and cheer. In Romania, people moved through their daily chores, weighed down by an invisible, ever-present load.

At the border, we had had to get off the train and open our suitcases for inspection. We had brought with us some bananas and a pineapple, exotic fruits in Romania. The customs man wanted to see what was inside the pineapple. It took a prolonged effort for my parents to finally convince him that this was a harmless fruit that would only spoil if it were cut open. A customs woman asked my mother to undress behind a curtain so she could be searched. There was tension in the air.

* * *

Unbeknownst to me, the newly imposed Communist regime was seeking to arrest my father. Before our return to Romania, an associate of my grandfather had called him and tried to warn him of the changes in the country: "Your wife is sick. She should not return too soon," he advised. "She should get medical treatment in Switzerland." My father was stunned. "What sick? What medical treatment? The man is nuts!"

"Maybe he is trying to tell us something," my mother suggested. "Maybe we should wait a while before we return."

My father would not hear of it. He belonged in Romania, whatever the situation there. That was his country, his family, his work, his duty. His place was "on the barricades." We had to return.

As the train was approaching the Romanian border, my mother kept on asking my father to get off the train and remain in the West. "Thirty more minutes to the border, let's get off . . . ten more minutes to the border . . ." My father thought about formalities: our visas for Switzerland had expired, where would we go if we got off? My mother thought about seeking political asylum, using our ties to Erna Kaeser, a devoted family friend working for the Swiss police in Bern.

We did not get off. As soon as the train stopped at the Romanian border town, Curtici, the loudspeakers started blaring: "The Popa family is to get off the train! The Popa family off the train!" Popa—that was us!

Mr. Bickman, the director of the Bumbacu branch in nearby Timişoara (the Swiss-originated textile enterprise in which my father was an officer), came to get my mother, my sister, and me. My father spent the night in Curtici, where our belongings were thoroughly searched, and much was stolen. The officials found financial arrangements my father had jotted on a piece of paper. When asked what they were, he said: "It's a memo on vitamins I purchased," and he was let go. The next day he jumped on the step of a train engine and joined us in Timişoara. From there we reached Bucharest together. That was the month of August 1947.

For the rest of her life, my mother was to regret the decision to return to Romania. Decades later, she was still second-guessing what our lives would have been like had we not returned.

Terror Settles In

Sometime after our return to Bucharest from our trip to Italy, my mother adopted an unusual ceremony: every evening she would light the candle beneath the icon in her bedroom and my little sister and I would kneel in front of it with her. We would all pray for our father's safe return from his business trip.

"Since when do we have to pray like that for a return from a business trip?" I wondered, somewhat irreverently. It is true that mother could sometimes be dramatic about trips. I remembered her anxiety about my father being cold on an upcoming trip for which he had packed a heavy winter coat and boots, all lined with a thick layer of sheep's fur. He was going to Moscow, and there seemed to be something ominous about that.

In the early, cold months of that year, before our trip to Italy, my father had accompanied a Romanian government trade commission to Moscow as a young expert in textile manufacturing. Its mission was to close a deal between Romania and the Soviet Union regarding, in particular, the processing of Soviet cotton in Romania. The commission was led by Gheorghe Gheorghiu-Dej, who held an important position in the recently imposed Communist regime. He was secretary-general of the Romanian Communist Party and an ally of Moscow.

To my father's surprise, however, Gheorghiu-Dej urged the group not to give in to all the Soviet demands but, rather, to defend Romania's interests. For my father, the point of contention was the percentage of weight loss that occurred in the processing of cotton, when some of the cotton turns into dust. My father was pressing for a weight loss as close as possible to its actual value, about 5%, whereas the Soviets wanted to base the negotiation on a much lesser loss, about 2%, which would have been to their advantage. Considering the deal to be unfair to Romania, after days of intense negotiations lasting well into the night and despite implied threats of unpleasant consequences were he to refuse to sign, my father stood his ground and refused to sign. He was the only one to do so (which may explain the reason for my father's next arrest, in October 1947, and my mother's prayers with a lit candle for his return).

After his return from Moscow, my father started having factory-related legal problems initiated by the government. "They are after you," the president of the Trade Council had warned him sometime after his return from Moscow. The regime's procedure was to pick people up during unexpected visits to their homes, preferably at night.

Now, duly warned after our reentry in Romania in August, my father stayed away from home until an official summons arrived in October from the Interior Ministry—one he could not ignore. When he showed up at the Ministry, he was arrested and held there for several weeks, sleeping on the floor, together with respected university professors and an ace aviator who caused a furor by managing to slip away and escape to the West. Women's screams in adjacent rooms were said to come from wives whose husbands refused to "talk."

From there my father was transferred to Jilava prison, a former fort near Bucharest that had been transformed into a penitentiary. There he joined engineers, lawyers, many members of the previous government, and some very well-known industrialists, sneeringly referred to as "saboteur gentlemen." My father was kept there until the day of his trial a couple of months later. Falsely accused of sabotage for weaving fabric with fewer threads per centimeter than required, my father brought in a textile expert who proved irrefutably that the accusation was false. He was defended by lawyers called in by my grandfather; this was a courageous act on their part.

One of them was Aurelian Bentoiu, former District Undersecretary of State for Justice and the Interior, then Attorney General in the government preceding the Soviet occupation. He was reputed for his knowledge as well as for his integrity. A year after my father's trial, Bentoiu himself was imprisoned, and eventually he died at Jilava.[7]

My father was finally acquitted by a judge who was friends with the husband of my grandfather's sister, Tanţa Rarinca, and set free in December 1947. Two or three days after his release, government commissars expelled my father and the other directors from the management of Industria Bumbacului. My father was replaced as CEO by a commissar (an official of the Communist party).

About six months later, a group of workers came to complain bitterly to my father and ask him to come back, saying they could not live in the new circumstances. Whereas, before, workers were paid for overtime, now they had to put in two to three free overtime hours daily: one for the Communist party, one for the Communists in Korea, one for indoctrination, and so on. In addition, they no longer had access to the clothing and food that had been provided at very low prices (such as inexpensive meat from cattle brought in from Transylvania) nor to the free medical care provided by four doctors (one of them was my father's brother Arnold) at clinics set up especially for workers and their families.

On June 11, 1948, all industry was nationalized. Groups of government people arrived at one o'clock in the morning and took over the family factories. My father was in Bucharest then, but his brother Valter was evicted from the factory at Constanţa. He was not allowed to remove documents from the safe deposit box.

---

[7]Cezarina Adamescu, "*Memento. Lungul drum al crucii spre lumină, Aurelian Bentoiu - 45 de ani de la proba demnităţii supreme*" (NOUA ARHIVĂ ROMÂNEASCĂ, on-line magazine). Also in the archives of "*Memorialul Victimelor Comunismului şi al Rezistenţei*" in Sighet, Romania.

Signs of Ever-Increasing Alarm

After my father returned from his "business trip," in 1947, the air filled with whispered stories of the black police car stopping in the darkest hours of the night and whisking people away, blindfolded so they would not know where they were being led. If family members tried to discover their whereabouts and succeeded, just to bring them food and clothing, they endured long waits at the prison where their loved ones were detained. My mother spent hours in my father's study checking through the pages of every single book of his vast collection to remove foreign banknotes that may have strayed there. Searches were now being made in people's homes for hidden currency, gold, guns, all of which became strictly forbidden by the Communist government.

The telephone turned into an instrument of fear. When it rang, the adults froze. Then followed frantic whispers to decide who should answer and what they should say if the police were calling. I was not used to seeing fear in adults' faces. Normally, children are frightened and adults reassure them. The world seemed upside down.

The same frightened expression paralyzed their faces when they found me scratching out ugly graffiti slapped with black paint on our bright, whitewashed wall by the sidewalk. I was told with urgency not to touch that paint: the graffiti represented the sun, the symbol of the Communist party.

Whispers of Escape Plans

There was whispered speculation about clandestine ways of leaving the country, about possible escape routes on the Black Sea, about men dyeing their hair blond to blend in with the crew of Swedish ships in the port of Constanţa so they could leave with them, and about expert swimmers hoping to reach, underwater, a foreign ship stationed in the port. That described my cousin Fred, who, at age five, had already weaved underwater like a fish.

> Indeed, as a twenty-year-old medical student, Fred attempted such an escape by sea. When he did not return home, his family did not dare alert the police in case he had decided to put his plan into action. Eventually, the police presented his family with a picture of a bloated corpse found, they said, on a beach by the border with Bulgaria. The features were unrecognizable. They also handed the family two pieces of underwear, one of them bearing Fred's initials. His family was not allowed to see the remains nor to bury them. Fred was never heard from again.

In time, as a precaution against the Soviet troops taking over our house, my parents arranged for a family of Swedish diplomats to move in, occupying the first floor and the two bedrooms on the second floor.

Alexe, a carpenter, built a wooden partition that separated our quarters from those of the Swedish family. This partition cut us off from the stairway where, at Christmas time, Anca, Tudor, and I used to eagerly await Santa Claus's arrival on the floor below. Also no longer accessible was the tiny balcony on the second floor where my mother had told me about the stars and astronomy, where she had pointed to the full moon, so clear that its shadows almost spoke to us, and had sung: "*Luna ştie, dar nu spune, multe taine din trecut.*" ("The moon knows, but does not share, many secrets from the past.") That's when I decided on the spot to become an astronomer and find out what the moon knew.

We were cut off as well from the piano and many of the rooms where we had lived and played, but I don't remember questioning our retrenchment. I accepted it, just as I accepted the pervading sense of sadness, without understanding very well its reason.

We Lose the Symbol of Our Nation, Our Only Protector

Matters much weightier than the partition seemed to absorb the adults. My parents now occupied the parlor and huddled around the radio at night. One evening, their voices were particularly hushed and a loaded silence sat heavy in the air. I had taken a shower in the little bathroom adjoining the parlor, and, wrapped in a towel, I tiptoed out. The radio was turned low. My parents were glued to it and whispered to each other. Consternation filled the room as they told me: "The king has abdicated."

King Michael

King Michael. The handsome, serious-looking young king who, more than anyone else, represented our country and stood up for us all. He had abdicated.

There was a sense of tremendous anxiety, of foreboding and gloom. Our leader, our only remaining hope against the intrusion of Soviet soldiers in our streets and in our homes, against the fear that now permeated our lives, had been forced to abdicate. We were now lost, abandoned at the total mercy of the invading Soviet troops. There was a feeling of sinking. A captainless ship adrift on an ominous sea.

"Rape"

Throughout all this turmoil, I continued being home-schooled so as not to be exposed to the Marxist–Leninist indoctrination now mandatory in education. Mrs. Livianu was preparing me for the end-of-year exams. I was to take the exams at school and I had to be very careful about what I would say.

After Soviet tanks poured into Romania in 1944, the Soviets imposed a Communist government in the country. It gradually took control of all aspects of life. In reaction to this takeover, a huge demonstration ensued. On November 8, 1945, the king's name day (known as Saint Michael's feast day on the Eastern Orthodox calendar), thousands of people gathered in the square in front of the king's palace in support of the king and to rail against the Communist government. The demonstrators were attacked with crowbars and shot at from the Interior Ministry on the opposite side of the square. There were casualties and hundreds of arrests.*

In the summer of 1947, about 2,000 opposition politicians, intellectuals, and workers were arrested in addition to the leaders of the traditional parties.** Members of the present government who did not strictly adhere to the Communist platform were forced to resign. Many were put on trial on trumped-up charges, condemned and imprisoned for years.

Iuliu Maniu, former prime minister, head of the National Peasant party and one of the most revered personalities of twentieth-century Romania, had pressed for equal rights for Romanians in Transylvania under the Austro-Hungarian empire and became a major player in the formation of modern Romania. After a show trial in November 1947, he was incarcerated for espionage and treason at the Sighet penitentiary in Northern Romania, in the direst of conditions. After six years of mistreatment, he died in isolation, alone in his cell, at age 80 years.†

In December 1947, the Soviet-imposed prime-minister, Petru Groza, compelled 26-year-old King Michael to abdicate by threatening him with the execution of 1,000 students who had been arrested during the demonstrations of November 1945.‡

*_Memorial Sighet, 8 Noiembrie 1945,_ Fundaţia Academia Civică – Memorialul Victimelor Comunismului şi al Rezistenţei.

**Keith Hitchkins, _The Oxford History of Modern Europe Rumania 18661947_, Clarendon Press, Oxford, 1994, pp. 540–545.

†_România Liberă_, Feb. 3, 2011.

‡Mircea Ciobanu "_Convorbitri cu Mihai I al României_" _Humanitas_, Bucharest, 1992, p. 59.

It was rumored that the parents of children who had repeated what they had heard at home had been imprisoned. I had been taught at home that our country was Romania and that our leader was King Michael, but at school I was to say that our country was the Romanian Socialist Republic and that our "beloved" leader was Stalin.

I shuddered at the thought of those repulsive, khaki-clad soldiers who spoke Stalin's barbaric language. A deep, shattering, screaming revolt bursts within me even now at the recollection and the only word that comes to my adult mind is: rape.

Rape. I did not know the word as a child, but I felt raped. I felt raped in the most intimate part of my being, the most sacred confines of my identity. Because of the Soviet troops, we could not say what we thought, we could not listen to what we chose, we were not "at home" in our own home. Our walls were defaced, and we could not restore them. The entire household was paralyzed by the ring of a phone. The adults seemed terrified and helpless. And I was required to say that Stalin was our beloved leader.

In a sense, this was worse than a physical assault. It was the laceration of our personhood, the devastation of our souls.

3

ESCAPE

AUGUST 1948

My scalded foot propped up, I was lying on the parlor couch, my parents by my side. "Do you think this is an omen?" my mother asked my father in a low voice.

"An omen of what?" I wondered. Mother had been melting an intriguing pink cream over a pot of boiling water she had placed on a hot plate on the floor. She was spreading the cream on her legs and, after it cooled off and hardened, she was slowly peeling it off. That apparently was meant to clear her legs of hair. I found the procedure fascinating and got closer and closer to the wondrous cream when, accidentally, the boiling water spilled and scalded my foot. The pain was intense, but I was used to pain what with the countless knee scratches and head bumps amassed in exuberant games with Tudor and Anca and borne stoically so as not to be any less brave than they were. More arresting was the transformation of the scalded area. The flesh had turned purple, the skin was peeling, and my foot had to be wrapped in many layers of gauze, topped with a black stocking.

It was with this impressive dressing that we left for our excursion on the Danube. Travel was restricted now even within the country, so we had to obtain special permission to go to Băile Herculane, ancient Roman hot springs on the shore of the Danube, to treat my mother's rheumatism. We each took along a backpack matching our size, from my father's huge contraption to my sister's tiny bag that would fit her potty and no more. She was three years old now and needed it at night.

The day after our arrival at Băile Herculane we set out for the river-bank. The Danube was very wide and carried opaque, beige waters. A launch was to pick us up for a ride and an afternoon picnic at the "Cazane" narrows. But first we sat down for lunch at a long, shady table that could accommodate all our party. It consisted of the four of us, a family with three sons roughly my age, an older couple, Nina and Stefan Besi (a Greek maritime agent associate of my grandfather),[8] and another couple. We ate fish, talked and laughed, children and adults alike, and made a very cheerful bunch, all except my father and the lanky Mr. Besi. The two of them stood apart in the shade of a tree, not far from our table, almost motionless, their faces drained of color. Why did they not eat? Why did they not join us? Perhaps Mr. Besi, like my father, was always serious and prone to worry, I thought.

When the launch arrived, we ran to climb on the benches from which we could watch the water flow. A sandy curve in the shore that jutted into the water was to be the site of our picnic. We stepped off the boat, we children played and explored while the adults drank beer and wine. Even though he partook in our food, the burly skipper was none too friendly. There seemed to be a scuffle between him and the shipmates after we returned on board. Tension filled the air. After a while, the launch came to a standstill on the other side of the Danube, amidst what seemed to me uncertainty and anxiety. I heard this was Yugoslavia.

How the Plans Went Awry

For years my mother would recount the story of our escape from Romania:

---

[8]He represented large shipping lines on which my grandfather was transporting goods such as, for example, jute from India for the manufacture of jute sacks.

The country had now been turned into a huge prison camp. There were massive arrests, private enterprise was outlawed, travel severely restricted. The months of my father's incarceration at Jilava, the takeover of his family's textile mills, the loss of his means of livelihood and compelling indications that he would be arrested again finally overcame my father's extreme caution and his sense that duty impelled him to stay in Romania. With the blessing of his father, the only one privy to his intentions, and strongly encouraged by my mother, who contacted my father's connections to obtain valuable dollars for an escape, my father arranged a clandestine crossing of the Danube into Yugoslavia, the only neighboring country free of Soviet troops because of the special relationship of its leader, Josip Broz Tito, with Stalin.

In Yugoslavia, a man with a cart was to pick us up and guide us through that country to Trieste in Italy. At the last moment, however, the owner of the boat did not show up. In his stead appeared his brother, a stern, hefty boatman, staunchly Communist, who would not hear of taking us across to Yugoslavia. He would only take us for a ride on the Danube.

When we stopped for the picnic, my parents and the other members of the party kept filling the boatman's glass with beer and wine, even dropping a sleeping pill in his drink. But nothing would daze this massive creature and no arguing would change his mind.

When the three young shipmates grasped our intention, they decided, on the spot, to escape with us. This meant a total disconnect from their families and friends, even the very real impossibility of informing them of their whereabouts.

Struggling for control of the boat with the skipper, who dwarfed them, and being unable to overpower him, the mates severed the connection between the wheel and the rudder. The strong Danube currents angling toward the Yugoslav shore carried along our drifting boat.

The Danube at the Iron Gates narrows.

Meanwhile, perhaps noticing our unusual maneuvers, a motor boat of the border patrol started racing toward us. Before they could reach us, however, our launch touched the Yugoslav shore. (We heard later that after our escape all excursions on the Danube were prohibited.)

On the shore, however, there was no cart to be seen.

Yugoslavia

For a reason I did not understand, we lined up and prepared to land. Why were we getting off? Were we leaving Romania again? No one explained, no one discussed our landing. The adults' faces were closed to my inquiring eyes, but they acted as if this course of action had been preordained. Slowly and carefully we stepped off the launch onto the Yugoslav shore.

As we all stood there waiting, I stared at the Romanian side. A deep, pervading, incomprehensible feeling of loss grabbed me: Will we ever go back to the Romanian side? Will I ever see my home again?

There was no asking, no understanding. I simply drifted along with the massive swell that changed the course of our lives. A cloud cover darkened the daylight. Or was it rather the tension of the adults?

Often while in prison and later in the Free World, I wondered about that moment when we disembarked in Yugoslavia—about the pervading sense of deep severance, of sinking, of overhanging gloom, as if I were watching Romania and all my world drift away, escape my reach, perhaps for a long, a very long time. (Thirty-five years later, I still feel an indescribably aching longing for that shore across the river, for our home, for our people, for my friends, for my grandparents, for the love and warmth that enveloped and nourished me there—all totally out of reach, a pain that deepened with the passing years.)

As we waited on the Yugoslav shore, young men in uniform came to meet us. The adults engaged in explanations. The moment felt awkward, perhaps because of the language barrier, perhaps for other

My grandparents, Elise and Apostol Popa, around the time of our escape.

reasons. We were escorted to a peasant home, like the one in which we had taken refuge in Romania during the war.

In Romania, we had had our meals outdoors, sheltered under low, leafy branches, with the exquisite aroma of lovage rising from the evening soup. This small, whitewashed dwelling in Yugoslavia felt just as cozy and welcoming, snuggled among lush trees that shaded a long table set for dinner. It looked ready for a party. I started to feel hungry, but the meal was not intended for us. We did not belong there. We belonged in Romania.

We settled in the yard for the night. We lay on the ground, amidst myriad mosquitoes that kept me squirming and scratching until I finally fell asleep. The captain of the ship, overcome now by the drinks he had been poured, snored on a nearby bench. He would not move until the next morning, when he requested to return to Romania.

The next morning, the guards took us by boat to a large city. I overheard the name "Belgrade." My mother was in bubbly spirits: "We must send a telegram to President Tito and thank him!" she proposed enthusiastically. "For what?" I wondered. The other adults seemed more skeptical and did not share her eagerness. Later I learned that her fear had been that Tito would send us back to Romania. This was one of the most dreaded outcomes because of the punishment the Romanian Communist government would inflict on us, with dire consequences for our families as well. My mother was grateful we were spared this fate.

We reached Belgrade after dusk had set in and, like a disquieting, hazy dream, I recall our walking along dark, unfamiliar streets in an unknown city toward an undisclosed destination. I don't remember where we spent the night. The next day we arrived by train at Kovačica.

4
PRISON IN KOVAČICA

We arrived at Kovačica by daylight. It was in the countryside, past a hamlet, amidst open fields lit by the warm, golden glow of a late August day. The dirt road led to a gated wall. Past the gate, in the middle of a courtyard enclosed on all sides by a thick, high wall, stood a small two-story building, drab and dilapidated.

"Where are we?" I inquired.

Mother must have felt uneasy, even worried, for she spoke in that semi-calm, semi-absent tone of voice that told me something was amiss: "It's a hotel."

A hotel? I had been in hotels in Italy and, just two days earlier, at Băile Herculane. No hotel had looked like that. Something had to be quite wrong if my mother was concealing the truth.

The interior of the building was dark. I could distinguish a stairway leading to the second floor, where the men were led. To the left, a partition made of iron bars marked the entrance to a minuscule hallway where a beam of daylight slipped through the crack of a metal door. The door opened into a small enclosure with sun rays squeezing through a small window way up on the wall, secured by more bars. All around, gray, bare walls. On the floor, straw. Nothing else. The thick door closed behind us.

Why was the door so thick? Why did it have that tiny little hole toward the top? Was it locked? I didn't know, but I was not sure it mattered, for the door seemed so heavy I doubted we could push it open even if it were unlocked.

"You're resisting. Tell us about prison. Were there no people there? No names? No faces? You're not mentioning anyone." said the moderator of the Dreikurs workshop retreat in Boulder decades later, when I attempted to understand my reaction to incarceration.

I don't remember anyone at the time of our arrival. Eventually, the small cell was filled with about a dozen women and five children, including my sister and me.

The iron door was not locked and could be pushed open. It was not that bad. The straw on the floor was novel, reminding me of my uncle's farm at Constanţa and the myriad adorable, irresistible little chicks that struggled to walk on straw and that I was not allowed to take them home to Bucharest.

The women lay down on the straw to nap. Nap. I had always disliked naps. They were so boring.

Now, in the cell, I couldn't sleep, of course. I watched the women cover their bare arms and faces with scarves, sweaters, or whatever was at hand, spending their nap time fending off the ubiquitous black, sticky flies that settled on us as soon as we stopped moving, pulling their protective cover from neck to face, to arms, to shoulders, to face again.

My father was locked upstairs in the men's quarters. We communicated with the men at mealtime, when we all lined up in the yard for food. But in between meals, my three-year-old sister's tiny size turned her into our personal messenger. She alone could slip, head and all, through the bars that secured our hallway from the rest of the building. Then, under our encouraging gaze, lithe and sprightly like a little elf, she would slowly climb the steps to the second floor where the men were locked behind another set of bars. There she would deliver to my father messages scribbled on a scrap of paper that asked, for example, "How are you?" I suspect she enjoyed the attention and her role as a go-between, doing what no one else could do during those hours when we were all locked up.

Those hours must have been fewer for us children than for the adults, for as I look back in my mind's eye at Kovačica, I see us roaming in the courtyard while the adults were kept inside. The yard was our playground, even though it offered little entertainment because we were warned to stay away from the well and the ground dirt was too dense to dig.

The fun was to be had on Sundays when the adults were let out all day and the boys and I entered exhilarating races with good-natured Banu Darvari, an adult whose mien filled with laughter and mischief as he played with us. He loved to tease me and gave me the hardest time at tag, being an expert at cutting short his dash and changing direction with a speed that left me breathless. I practiced his tactics over and over but never quite succeeded in catching him. However, the boys could never catch me thereafter.

As autumn progressed and more arrivals joined us, the men became packed like sardines, as Naum Neagoe, who shared my father's cell, described with his perennial sense of humor: they slept on their sides and when one man wanted to turn on the other side, all had to turn over in unison!

One memorable arrival brought to our prison a towering, heavy-set man dressed all in black, with an ugly, frightening disposition. He was said to be Father Burducea, a former priest turned Communist and a member of the Communist government until he fell out of grace with the party. He had escaped from Romania with his wife and his twenty-year-old daughter, who, in sharp contrast to him, looked gentle and friendly.

They had barely set foot at Kovačica when he started pouring out his fury, haranguing us with a bellowing voice: "The Communists are too kind to you!" he glowered. "If I were in their shoes, I would have you all lined up against this wall and shot!"

I shrank inwardly, trying to resist the fear that was grabbing me.

"He is not allowed to have a gun," I tried to reassure myself. "He is a prisoner, just like the rest of us." Still, I felt shaken by his shouts. And amazed. He shared our plight, we were all locked up on the same side of the wall, we were all at the mercy of our jailers. Why was he so violent against us when he barely knew us? And if he was locked up by the Communists, why was he talking like a Communist? And if he was a Communist, why was he locked up?

Subsequent waves of arrivals swelled the ranks of the women too. Young women, including pregnant women, filled our cell just as the men had filled the cells upstairs.

Pregnancy was a very present issue in those days, especially in connection with food. Hunger became more intense as time went by. Our standard regimen of a cup of sweetened chicory coffee in the morning with a piece of bread to last the whole day, a cup of barley soup or pea soup for lunch and for dinner hardly appeased our hunger. (The pea soup consisted of a clear liquid with, on average (I liked to count), 7 peas, each containing a black bug I would carefully remove.)

Fainting

There was talk of milk and additional nourishment for pregnant women. When we lined up to return to our cells at night, one or another of the young women would start to lose her balance or "faint" as the adults referred to it. Some people were concerned for them, others were making fun of them, implying they were faking pregnancy in the hope of more food. Whatever the case may have been, we never received more food, not for the pregnant women nor for anyone else.

But "faint"—that intriguing word—was how my mother described me one morning. The night before, I had had one of those dreams I was so longing for, a wondrous dream that would allow me for at least a few minutes to relish the impossible. A dream of food for which I had intensely wished but that never visited me.

That night, or perhaps I should say that morning, I dreamt I held a cracker in my hand. I can still see that cracker, the lovely roundedness of the scalloped edges, the tiny decorative holes, the honey color foretelling the sweet, rich taste that would fill my stomach with warmth and coziness and start to appease my hunger. As I was about to slowly bite into it and savor its texture, the morning sun slid its rays between the bars and drew me back to reality. I became conscious of the straw about me and the cracker faded in my hand before I had a chance to press my teeth into it. It was a dream. Only a dream.

I focused on that dream with all my might, the feel of the cracker, the taste of that first bite I never had—but I could not recapture it. I got up, ready to start the day, but stopped short: I felt dizzy and could not move. I lay down again. "What is it, mother? Why do I feel dizzy?"

To my acute embarrassment, mother started lamenting about my feeling "faint" and something about hunger. They took me outside and laid me on the large table in the yard. The weather was mild, the sun bright and warm and its rays slanted toward the back of my head.

Suddenly, the light was blocked—someone had come between the sun and the table. I looked up and saw a lock of black hair curling gracefully on a fair forehead: it was the handsome young man, so gentle and kind, on whom I had developed a crush! Alas, he was forever walking with Dana, a slender, attractive, and flirty blonde with blue-green eyes. There was talk of marriage between them, not "for real" but for convenience. He was believed to have a good chance of being sent to work and she wanted to leave prison with him as his wife. After weeks of eating and sleeping on the floor with some twenty other women and children, the lure of work, as I fancied it, was a room of one's own, with a bed, a table, and a chair to sit on. Now he was standing at the end of the table, lowering his gentle, caring gaze toward me. I looked at him, he smiled, then, softly, bent over and kissed my forehead.

He kissed me! That lit my entire day. The dizzy spell had almost been worthwhile.

Eventually he did leave the prison, but without Dana. The priests who were among us refused to go along with their stratagem: they would perform only religiously meaningful ceremonies.

The Priests

Two priests had been brought in during the warm days, an elderly one, Father Vasile Leu, and a younger one, Father Florian Gâldău. They both wore beards in the Eastern Orthodox tradition. Father Gâldău's was dark and short. Father Leu's was white, long, flowing, beautiful. His face radiated kindness and compassion. If God had a face, I thought, it was surely like Father Leu's.

Every Sunday we would gather around the priests in the courtyard and they would preach. I remember mostly Father Leu. His sermons were the highlight of the week. He spoke slowly and clearly, and what he said was within my reach, even though I was only eight. I drank his words. They seemed to flow from his soul. They were filled with notions of love, patience, courage, strength, understanding, compassion, forgiveness. They soothed us and fed us. We were so hungry in every way and his words were our greatest solace. I marvel now, as an adult, that anyone could evoke such sentiments in the grim and heartless setting of our everyday life with armed guards pacing on top of the wall and all we knew were guns and hunger. Was it weakness on their part?

We were soon to discover it was strength, and their strength was surprisingly daring.

Cesspool

When we were all locked inside, we could still leave our cell, for the unlocked heavy door opened into a very small hallway. One end of it was confined by bars, the other by a wall. To the left of the wall, the hall opened into a small space with a window. Within that space there was a toilet, enclosed on three sides, but with no door for privacy. The seat had an incredible assortment of colors all over it for it was smeared with excrement. There was a hole in the ceiling above it and a hole in the floor below. I was afraid someone on the floor above might be using the latrine through the upper hole while I was using the one below. I had to climb on the filthy, slippery seat for I was too short to use the toilet otherwise and, every time, I fought the fear of falling into it. Through the hole one could see, eerily lit by daylight coming from below, the glittering colors of a vast cesspool.

It was a big, bright, shiny, threatening cesspool, about the size of a two-car garage. From the yard one could see the large double doors that afforded access to it. When the doors were open, I would be mesmerized by the sea of reds and greens and browns of the moist feces. It was a shock. The brilliant, glistening colors scared me and yet I could not put them out of my mind. They held the fascination of an object of fright that I did not know how to handle. I mentally stared at it to keep it at bay, to make certain it would not catch up with me as I turned my back on it, and in time that cesspool became my nightmare.

I struggled to resist visions of falling into that multicolored mass, gasping for air, scrambling not to drown, just as I struggle now to stay above Kovačica, above prison, above the frightening wave of excrement that engulfed my childhood world and my country of birth, which terrifies me and yet on which I cannot turn my back. How does one extricate oneself—and others—from that vast cesspool of human suffering, from the torture and the killings, from the ugliness of man-inflicted torment and oppression?

What I dreaded befell a little dog that had arrived with Yvonne Băleanu. The adults seemed struck by Yvonne's beauty. She was quite plump, but had a luminous, white complexion, huge black eyes and rich, long, lustrous black hair. This, I suspected, was what impressed the adults. I liked her because she was very gentle.

Yvonne had escaped with her elderly mother who, in contrast, was thin, dry, and sickly. Yvonne worried about her. One day she approached the prison's commander, told him about her mother's health problems and asked him for medical assistance. He reportedly went to the window and pointed to a plot beyond the dirt road: "The cemetery is across the way."

The women in the cell were quite shocked by this answer. They did not discuss its implications, but they were clear: "You live by your own means or you die"—a disquieting lesson I carried, subconsciously, into adulthood.

Yvonne had brought along a little brown, short-haired dog. It was a totally unexpected presence, since most of us had escaped only with the clothes on our backs and what fit in a bag the size of a backpack. Even this was a luxury, as became obvious when newcomers shared the experience of their escapes. Those who braved the punishing Danube currents swam for hours on end, sometimes underwater to escape detection. They most often had to drop whatever belongings they were dragging along and reached the shores of Yugoslavia at best in shorts. Naum Neagoe, with his perennial good spirits, laughed as he was telling me how he had lost his underwear as well to the famous Danube eddies and met the Yugoslav border guards stark naked. To cover him up, they had given him a heavy woolen coat complete with bullet holes and blood stains. I think my jaw dropped as the story's full implication sank into my consciousness.

Yvonne's dog was therefore quite incongruous in that setting. The guards were prompt to turn that rare occasion into what was, for them, some fun: they grabbed the dog and carried it away with a merry, mischievous expression, under Yvonne's concerned gaze. They returned it a little later, multi-colored and stinking: they had dropped it in the cesspool and retrieved it to present it in its full glory to his mistress. Yvonne's distress visibly heightened their amusement.

The closest I came to that fate was one day when I slipped and fell into the toilet. I don't remember how I pulled myself up, but my return to the cell was unforgettable: as I stood in the doorway, all the heads sprang up at once, alerted by what must have been an overpowering stench. My white woolen panties were smeared all over. While the other women winced in disapproving disgust, my mother, all love and tenderness and compassion, came and cleaned me up. How she cleaned me, I don't know, because I don't remember ever washing. But perhaps in those early days we had some water from the deep, narrow well in the yard.

Washing /Drinking Water

Our drinking water came from town. A handful of prisoners, led by guards, would each carry two large metal pails to the village well. They would bring the full pails back, bending under their weight, careful not to spill, wincing with pain from the metal handle that cut into their bare hands. Once, when winter had settled in and the cold was bitter, I saw my father returning from one of these expeditions. The sight of his swollen fingers, reddened by the cold, slashed white at the knuckles by the freezing handles on which he strained to maintain a hold, frightened me. There is no way we could have washed with that precious drinking water.

Still, in winter, some people did wash—with water descended from heaven in the form of snow. About half a dozen daring men were out in the yard in the early hours of the morning. Decades later, I can still see this indelible sight—men bared to the waist, standing by a pile of snow stacked in a corner of the wall, picking up handfuls of the white, frozen fluff and rubbing it vigorously on their naked torso. One was my father. He stood out, very white and thin, his ribs almost showing under his skin, so frail and vulnerable. I watched them, incredulous, and shivered at the bare sight. It was beyond my understanding.

"How could you wash like that in those freezing temperatures?" I asked my father years later, in disbelief. "That's what kept us healthy," said my father. "That's what kept us healthy," would echo my mother, recalling the cloves of garlic and the onions on which we feasted once in the early fall days. They suddenly appeared on the large courtyard table when it was still warm. It was one of those unique, inexplicable happenings, a wondrous apparition. I never thought to ask my parents, years later, where the onions and garlic came from. With his hands, an adult would press a large white onion against the table's edge until it burst open, releasing its tender, juicy meat and we could soak in its moist sweetness and quench our deep hunger with its appeasing fullness. Then we would take a slice of bread and toast it over the flame of burning wood and rub a clove of garlic all over it, savoring its aroma as we slowly chewed the bread and swallowed it. A glorious feast, but ephemeral like a fairy tale, for it did not last long.

The Tailor

In a little cell across from ours lived a tailor, all by himself. Like us, he was a prisoner, but he was granted favored treatment for reasons that remained a mystery and, of course, arose suspicion. The guards would visit him regularly, sharing food and lighthearted banter.

One evening the guards came into our cell and asked me to join them. The invitation pleased me for I was curious. Not so the women. Their apprehension was almost palpable, for whatever reason I couldn't grasp at the time.

I followed the guards to the tailor's cell where an unreal sight unfolded: chairs, a table, and on the table, under a lampshade, a yellow circle of light highlighting glasses, a bottle of wine and a plate. On the plate, a piece of meat.

The guards, young and carefree, sat merrily at the table. The tailor sat me on his lap. They poured a little wine in a glass and offered it to me together with bread and a piece of meat. I felt my stomach tighten shut. How could I possibly touch this meat when next door they had not seen meat since we arrived? Did this not bother the tailor? How could he feast with our guards when he must know the rest of us lived in deprivation? The guards were pleasant and seemed inoffensive, almost as if they had nothing to do with us. But they belonged on the other side of the bars and their job was to keep us locked.

My heart felt so heavy. I could not tell if they were trying to be nice to me or were simply having fun, but they kept on offering me a bite of meat, a sip of wine. I did not want to eat. I did not want to drink for it made me dizzy. But they kept on insisting, cheerfully, one more bite, one more sip of wine while they kept laughing and joking. I did not know there could be so much laughter in that prison.

When I finished the meat and emptied the glass of wine, they led me back to our cell. I couldn't walk straight. I didn't want the women in the cell to see me in such a condition. I felt myself zigzagging and made an enormous effort to advance slowly, to focus my mind and to remain alert to my surroundings. In our cell all eyes converged on me, my mother's face a big question mark. She did not have to ask, I could read it on her expression: "What happened? What did they do? Are you okay?"

I did not understand her fear. All was well.

Strike

As the weather turned cold, we children started spending more and more time inside with the adults. As usual, the men were locked upstairs. The priests would lead them in song. From the women's cell below, we would join our voices to theirs in verses that stirred our souls:

"*Cu noi este Dumnezeu... veniţi şi vă rugaţi: căci cu noi este Dumnezeu.*" ("God is with us. . . . Come all and pray, for God is with us.")

I remember this song with vibrant poignancy. Despite the bars, despite the walls, despite the guards, we could all join our voices and spirits and unite in a deep sense of communion, of shared grief. It gave us the comfort of a presence much greater than ours, it gave us courage and strength to continue bearing our plight without giving up hope.

At about that time, the men went on a hunger strike.

"What's a hunger strike?" I inquired.

My father explained that the men refused to eat until we got more decent treatment. That may have been the time when the toilets overflowed into the hallways, filling them with urine. We had to cross over on shaky, splashing boards. The stench was omnipresent, although now I remember it only intellectually. Perhaps the smell had become one with the sight.

So it was not difficult to understand why the strikers would yearn for improvements. But I could not understand why they would stop eating. We were already so hungry. That anyone should give up the little we had frightened me. What could make them act like that? What difference would it make? And for what? For the hope of better treatment? That was utter nonsense! What did our jailors care whether we ate or not? Who would know if we lived or died? Did anyone "on the outside" know we were here, cut off from all communication as we were? No letters, no telephone calls, no messages, no visits, nothing.

No one in the outside world was aware of our existence or our whereabouts, not even our families. Occasionally, new people would be brought in. Rarely, some would be taken out, to work. I felt we were relegated to complete, total, absolute isolation, existing "underground" so to speak, in a place lost to humanity. And now the men were going on a hunger strike. I felt both compassion and anxiety, almost as if their deeds were threatening me.

"They must be made aware of our rights," my father continued. Rights? The guards, the people who held us, could do whatever they wanted with us! What did he mean by *our rights*? I felt almost angry at father for not grasping our reality. We had no rights. We were to be counted and to be kept hidden. If we were lucky, we survived.

I think the outside world may have lost meaning for me by then. The adults spoke about it and once my mother had referred to it when she spoke of my going to school when we would be free. But with time the outside world was fading away and I was losing the sense of its reality.

There was the prison and the guards. Nothing else.

Perhaps God.

Invisible.

What was the use of hoping, of believing?

In fact, looking back on those years, I think the strike may have had an effect, for I don't remember the toilets overflowing again for longer than a limited time.

Madame Sunshine

Christmas was approaching. There was talk that perhaps at the Christmas season we might have an egg. Was it my mother's wishful thinking, she who was always pleading "for the children"? Was it a real possibility? We were all hoping. But as the days went by and our stomachs grew emptier and our longing deeper, our hope became more and more dim.

Still, there was to be an egg for Christmas, but not for us. At about that time we were joined in prison by an army general, a little mustachioed man as modest and effaced as his none-too-young wife was flashy, flirty, and vain. The adults mockingly nicknamed her "Madame Sunshine" for her reddish hair and the make-up she was forever adjusting on her flat, round face, the only woman, they observed, to flirt with the guards. To keep herself in shape, she asked us children to walk on her back as she lay prone on the straw. We had a delightful time indulging her wish, hanging onto our balance while she moaned and groaned under our gleeful steps, repeating with conviction, "This is good for me." The pain did not deter her.

Madame Sunshine's worldly concerns floated above the sparseness of our everyday surroundings—not surprisingly because she was the sole owner of a most quaint and extravagant possession: a sheet. A white sheet—the only sheet we ever saw in prison. And, of course, she guarded it vigilantly, just as she guarded her egg.

The egg for Christmas was Madame Sunshine's. I don't think we ever discovered how she procured it, but procure an egg she did. The adults managed not to pay too much attention to it, but we children were drawn to it like to a magnet, watching it sizzle, sunny side up, in a pan placed on our cell's wood stove. Not for long, though. Madame Sunshine quickly shooed us off, "Stay away! I don't want you to spread your germs on the egg!" We never saw her eat her egg.

Instead of an egg, I started dreaming of a little wooden cart. Somehow, an empty wooden spool had shown up. Perhaps brought by a woman who had no use for it once the thread was gone. Mother, the perennial optimist, lit up. "Look at that spool! Three more and we could make a cart for the children for Christmas!"

My heart leapt with joy. A toy for Christmas! Could that be possible?

Mother placed the spool on the windowsill, while waiting for the other three to appear. I would look at it during the day and imagine the little toy cart at night as I lay down to sleep. But there were to be no other spools and no toy cart built for Christmas.

Mother always thought the intention was what mattered, but that intention really hurt. I would much have preferred never to have hoped for the cart. With so much emptiness already, it was so sad to lose that hope too. There was no need to spur that useless hope, that hopeless dream. It would have been far better never to have hoped.

Along with hunger, a permanent sadness and resignation settled in. I don't remember any more leaps of joy or sudden hopes.

As Christmas drew nearer, mother asked the guards if we could have a Christmas tree, maybe go cut a spruce in the surrounding woods. The guards laughed.

We found among our blankets a green one, took it upstairs to the men's quarters where we were allowed to gather for that occasion and tacked it on the wall. That was to represent the huge Christmas tree that had always been mysteriously brought by Santa Claus into our living room in Romania.

Christmas

On Christmas Eve in Romania, the stairway in our house throbbed with intense suspense. A heavy metal door sealed the stairs halfway between upstairs and the ground floor as protection against the spread of fire. That's where we children waited with keen impatience for the arrival of Santa Claus downstairs.

Tudor, Anca, and I would press our ears on the door, but all was silence. We would take turns peeping through the deep, dark keyhole, but all was black. Over and over again, just as Tudor or Anca would suddenly catch a glimpse of Santa and I would rush to press my eye on the keyhole, the apparition was gone.

After what seemed like an interminable wait, the magic moment was at last at hand: the door turned slowly on its hinges, and, intimidated by the majesty of the event, we cautiously descended the remaining steps into the total darkness of the living room. As we turned our heads to the right, a gigantic Christmas tree appeared, rising all the way to the ceiling, shimmering with all the sparkle of its countless candles lit with real flames. The first strains of *Silent Night* emerged from the surrounding obscurity and the cry "Santa Claus has arrived!" rang into our ears. All else was silence and awe.

On Christmas Eve at Kovačica, we all gathered around the green blanket. Men, women and children sang the Christmas carols[9] we had learned over the past several weeks from Father Surducan, who had recently escaped from Romania with his wife and their seven-year-old son Victor, nicknamed "Puiu." Their family remained incarcerated with us almost until the end of our imprisonment there. (As one manifestation of trauma, Puiu confirmed to me decades later in a telephone conversation that he has no recollection whatsoever of his stay in prison.)

Priests' Escape

Not long after Christmas, we were gathered around the priests in a cell on the second floor. It was winter and too cold to be outdoors. The cell was small and cramped. The theme of their sermon was, as I recall, "Ask and you shall receive, knock and it shall be opened to you, dare and you shall succeed" (my recollection, not the standard biblical version). I remember these words, because people repeated them afterwards, stunned.

During that sermon, the priests had also asked for our forgiveness, should we have to suffer because of them. That was amazing to me. Forgive them? They were all kindness, giving, and love. What could we possibly have to forgive them?

Several days later, on the night of January 6, 1949 (the date Father Gâldău related to me several decades later[10]), we were awakened by a great commotion. The guards were running about, shouting, asking questions of us, half angry, half scared, it seemed. "What happened?" They would not answer. But the rumor quickly spread: the priests had escaped.

---

[9]See some of the carols at end of this chapter.

[10]From Father Gâldău's account of his amazing escape, as recorded by me in New York several decades later.

Escaped? The priests? No one had escaped from that prison, no one had ever mentioned a past escape, no one had ever heard of an escape. It was unthinkable. But if anyone were to escape, the priests were absolutely the last ones we would have expected to do so. Maybe the young man who had tried to scale the wall on the day of his arrival, maybe some hot-headed young people, but not the priests.

We were all incredulous, yet we wanted to believe the news as one wants to believe a fairy tale. As the minutes passed, the rumor seemed to turn into certainty: Father Leu, Father Gâldău, and a third man whom I did not know had escaped. They had apparently scaled the wall during the night. It had snowed, and their tracks could be seen on the fresh powder. But they hadn't been caught yet. How far could they go? Would they walk? Would they jump on a train? There was much talk about the different ways of riding on a train without being discovered: lying down on the roof, hiding in the coal car, hanging between the wheels, or moving from car to car to skirt control. Many had used these methods to escape from Romania and the stories abounded.

Would it be a matter of hours, of days, until the priests would be caught and returned to Kovačica? Or would they be imprisoned elsewhere?

There were already names with nightmarish connotations reaching my awareness: Panchevo, Ljubljana, the most dreaded prisons. Or could the priests possibly make it to the West? With all our might we were hoping for that outcome, even if no one had yet succeeded in escaping. We prayed fervently and hoped for their success and feared seeing them brought back to our prison. Or hearing of a worse fate.

The hours passed, the guards calmed down, but still no news of the priests. The day went by, and then the night, and still no news nor any rumors. Could they still be at large? That was incredible, for surely a countrywide hunt must have been organized by now. Could they evade the militia that long?

With each passing day our hope increased, until days turned into months and at last we trusted we would not hear from them nor see them again in our prison underworld. They must have made it to the West.[11]

The priests' escape was galvanizing. We sensed it as a victory in which we all shared, despite the loss it meant for us because now life was so empty without their sermons, without the hope, and the spirit of caring and decency they infused into our lives. I cannot imagine a higher spiritual impact on us than that of Father Leu and Father Gâldău. Their escape was their ultimate legacy of courage and hope for they showed us that prison was not invincible, that kindness and forgiveness did not mean weakness and defeat. "Ask and you shall receive, knock and it shall be opened to you, dare and you shall succeed." And they did. I wish that lesson had marked me more deeply. But that event occurred only a few months into our detention, and as time went on and on, the bleakness of our isolation permeated my soul and despair took over. I was growing up with a total sense of helplessness and, in time, of hopelessness.

Departure

It was still bitter cold when we were moved to Zrenianin, on a frigid winter night when we were led outside the prison walls. We had escaped to Yugoslavia in summer with just a backpack each. Now we bundled up as best we could in clothes picked from boxes that had arrived from the United States, blessing inwardly the Americans.

The only shoes to fit me were slightly tight. We started our long walk to the train station on snow-covered ground. The air was clear, the cold bitter and penetrating. Soon, my fingers and toes went numb.

Then, the pain started. In time, it became so intense I did not know how I could handle it, how I could go on walking with the biting,

[11] See Appendix D for an account of their escape.

unrelenting pain of cold. Hunger pangs come and recede. Cold is unyielding.

In Romania, I had prided myself on being brave and not giving in to hurt. Now, my courage was floundering.

Struggling alongside Comandorul Mircea Pătru,[12] I strained not to break down and cry. With his generous proportions and jolly disposition, he seemed both comfortable and cheerful. In other circumstances, just the sight of him would have warmed me up. But now, the road was too long and too harsh.

Comandorul encouraged me as best he could. He must have done wonders to soothe me, because in this protracted and painful march, his presence is the only one I remember.

At last we reached the train station and were herded into a cold, barren car the adults said was meant for cattle. Comandorul took my frozen hands and feet and held them tight against his ample belly, but the pain would not relent. Cold hangs on and releases its punishing grip with the greatest reluctance. Eventually, Comandorul's warmth, both physical and moral, overcame my discomfort.

---

[12]Mircea Pătru, 1903–1987, was a commander in the Romanian Air Force who had served in World War II. After the Soviet occupation of Romania, he escaped to Yugoslavia in 1949 and from there to Italy.

Christmas Carols Learned in Prison

Oh, What Wondrous News[13]

O, ce veste minunată,
Din Betleem ni s-arată.
Că a născut prunc
Prunc din Duhul Sfânt
Fecioara curată.

Oh, what wondrous news
Appears to us from Bethlehem.
That the Pure Virgin
Has borne a child
From the Holy Spirit.

Mergând Iosif cu Maria
La Betleem să se-nscrie.
Într-un mic sălaş
Lâng-acel oraş
S-a născut Mesia.

As Joseph and Mary went
To Bethlehem, for the census.
In a small shepherds' shelter,
Close to that town,
The Messiah was born.

Ce Domnul cel din vecie,
Ni l-a trimis ca să vie,
Să se nască
Şi să crească,
Să ne mântuiască.

Whom the Lord, who is before all ages,
Sent to us, so that He come,
To be born,
To grow up,
And to save us all.

[13]Translation by Cristian Mocanu, modified by Ingrid Popa Fotino.

Three Shepherds[14]

Trei păstori se întâlniră (bis)	Three shepherds met
Raza soarelui, floarea soarelui.	Sunbeam, sunflower.
Şi aşa se sfătuiră.	And talked to each other thus:
Haideţi, fraţilor, să mergem (bis)	Come on, brothers, let us go
Raza soarelui, floarea soarelui.	Sunbeam, sunflower.
Floricele să culegem.	And pick some little flowers.
Şi să facem o cunună (bis)	And make a crown out of them
Raza soarelui, floarea soarelui.	Sunbeam, sunflower.
S-o-mpletim cu voie bună.	And knit it joyfully.
Şi s-o ducem lui Cristos (bis)	And take the crown to Christ,
Raza soarelui, floarea soarelui.	Sunbeam, sunflower.
Să ne fie de folos.	For the good of us all.

[14]Verses from : http://www.versuri.ro/

The Star Rises

Steaua sus răsare
Ca o taină mare,
Steaua străluceşte
Şi lumii vesteşte.

Că astăzi Curata,
Preanevinovata,
Fecioara Maria
Naşte pe Mesia.

În ţara vestită
Betleem numită
Magii cum zăriră
Steaua şi porniră

Mergând după rază
Pe Hristos să-l vază
Şi dacă aflară
La Dânsul intrară

Cu daruri gătite
Lui Hristos menite
Având fiecare
Bucurie mare

Care bucurie
Şi la noi să fie
De la tinereţe
Pân-la bătrâneţe.

The Star rises in the sky
Like a boundless mystery.
The star that so sparkles,
To the world announces:

That today, the pure,
The most innocent,
The Virgin Maria
Gives birth to Messiah

In the renowned country
Bethlehem by name.
As soon as they saw it
The Magi got started ,

Following the beam,
To behold the Christ.
And as they discovered Him,
They entered His dwelling

Bearing special gifts
That are meant for Christ.
Each of them is filled
With the greatest joy.

Let such joyous feeling
Be with us as well,
Starting from our youth
Into our old age.

5

PRISON CAMP IN ZRENIANIN: TAKING ROOTS IN THE UNDERWORLD

"Why did you come back here?"
"To try and let it go. It's something that haunts me every day."

—Cpl. Steven Comfort as interviewed by Scott Pelley upon his return to the Iraqi battlefield, where he was severely wounded while trying to save his lieutenant.[15]

It haunted me also. I yearned to let go of the weight that had been dragging me down for so many years. To go back to Zrenianin, to the soil where my soul was pinned, to drop off the load that I cannot discard and with which I cannot live, and rest there forever.

* * *

On one of our family trips to Europe, Domnica exclaimed, "Let's go to Dachau!" as we were passing an arrow pointing to

[15]"Operation Proper Exit: A Return to the War Zone (CBS News, November 6, 2011).

the Nazi concentration camp on our way to Mozart's birthplace in Salzburg,

My heart shriveled. Adriana had just turned eight, my age when I entered Zrenianin. Dachau was the last place I wanted to go on this trip. We were traveling for relaxation and fun, not for flaring up half-healed wounds. But Domnica was both persistent and convincing. "I want to see if it was anything like your childhood, Mom!" We went to Dachau.

Somehow, Dachau felt almost like home to me. Home, as in "the place where we belong"; like Zrenianin, with its high wire fence enclosing a rectangular space and, in its midst, prison cells reminiscent of Kovačica.

In its essence, though, Zrenianin was nothing like Dachau, nothing like the unspeakable horror of the mass exterminations, nothing like the horrendous gas odor still lingering in the gas chambers, nothing like the pervasive, suffocating existential threat. But Dachau had the outward appearance of a prison camp and certain of its aspects looked so familiar they felt like a closing of the circle, back to the site where my soul was impaled and from which it cannot pull free.

Escorted by Mircea, the girls, and dear Romanian friends from Munich, I dared enter Dachau. Mercifully, crowds of tourists opened the space up to the outside world, as it were, ensuring that it would not suddenly slam tight, swallowing us in the underworld of my childhood.

As I shared recollections with our friends, I felt incredibly relieved of pain, more like a kind of appeased torment. I had lived in Zrenianin. I had grown there even if my whole being struggled to reject it, to deny it, to erase it. That's when I understood that one cannot cut off an entire part of one's life, no matter how painful, how repulsive. It makes us who we are. Without it,

I would be partly dead. It's this part of me that I must accept and integrate and even embrace, for it is my life, it is me.

* * *

Arrival at Zrenianin

The camp in Zrenianin opened up as a soothing, luminous oasis in our underworld, much less forbidding than the severely enclosed prison at Kovačica. Its wide yard lay all on one side of a two-story building, surrounded by a wire fence through which we could see instead of the tall wall that had cooped us up at Kovačica, and it allowed our gaze to wander over the barren fields. I could even imagine fitting my fingers and toes in its mesh and climbing over it. Like lungs expanding with air, the yard filled with a large ring of detainees, walking in pairs, men and women together, some arm in arm, around and around, engaged in civil conversation in this most incongruous of settings, for at Zrenianin we were all let out of our rooms the entire day.

The outhouses, relegated at the end of the yard, were a source of unhoped-for fun. The door to the women's outhouse had a hook for privacy, which the boys and I locked from the outside and watched as women waited for the person who was supposedly using it to come out. Then with a burst of laughter we revealed there was no one inside!

Birds

With the approach of spring, a whiff of fresh air penetrated our quarters. One morning, I woke up to a totally unheard-of sound, a sound belonging to storybooks or to a now unreal past: the sound of *birds*!

As the yard and the field beyond were totally barren, there were no birds around. Yet I was sure I had heard the chirping of birds. My mother would not be convinced: "There, mother, to the right, just now, did you hear that?" In utter disgust, deflating my enthusiasm, mother exclaimed: "Those are not birds, those are mice!" My spirits picked up right away: Mice? What joy! A toy to play with!

A cat had found its way amongst us, and it too delighted in mice. I discovered a dead mouse, picked it by the tail and, to my mother's horror (as a child, she had been traumatized by rats during World War I), I twirled it in front of the cat in spirited play. Not for long, though. The cat quickly tired of the game, stretched a lazy paw, then turned away, bored. Was she not hungry, like the rest of us? Or had she gorged on other mice?

Out of Siberia

Exposed now all day to the company of men as well as women, our universe expanded considerably. As we sat around on the ground and listened to their stories, we discovered that not having much to do was a blessing in disguise. We learned about forced labor, which so many of the men had endured in the harshest of conditions before coming to Zrenianin. They told hair-raising stories about the bitter cold in Siberia and people losing their noses and their ears to frostbite; about a group of prisoners who were saved by their leader when he whipped them into walking rather than allowing them to rest and freeze to death. There were those who had managed to secrete building materials to burn for warmth or barter for food. They said they would be amazed if those shoddily constructed buildings were still standing. (Years later, at the French high school I attended in New York, in keeping with a trend of idealizing the Soviet Union, my classmates and I would be taught about the "fantastic advances the Soviets had made in developing the barren lands of Siberia.")

Despite this impromptu education, I missed books and school immensely. Sometimes I sat on the ground in the yard and stared at the gate, aching for it to open and let in my friends Tudor and Anca, carrying with them the *Tales of Ispirescu*, fantastic children's tales that had captivated my imagination in Romania.

My mother attempted to teach me the intricacies of the Romanian preterit tense or the working of a bank, but the latter did me in. I felt dizzy and could not concentrate. I did handle, though, the mental exercise of bridge! This was played with a deck of cards fashioned from paper. I was even allowed to try my hand at it, to my mother's partners' utter lack of enthusiasm. But the game that captivated me was chess. My grandfather had promised, in Romania, to teach it to me "later." Now, with the arrival of Liliana and Sandu Economu, I had at last a chance to learn it.

The time to learn, though, was short. Within a few months, Liliana and Sandu would be buried in the mountains of Macedonia, together with their parents, shot dead by the Yugoslav guards.

Liliana and Sandu

The Economu family, including two teenagers, Liliana and Sandu, had been brought in just as we discovered a vast open space on the second floor of our building. It was a vacant expanse with glassless windows, a cross draft, and fresh gray cement all over. Someone had built a fire in its midst.

It became a "ballroom" when fifteen-year-old Liliana would sweep me in large waltz turns as she hummed with zest the tune of "The Waves of the Danube" (known in the United States as the "Anniversary Song"), which conjured the sway of water: "*Barca pe valuri plutește ușor*" ("The boat on the waves is floating so lightly").

Liliana's grace and her thick, long braid caught the adults' attention. Mother noted that the hue of Liliana's eyes matched exactly the dark honey color of her hair. Mother, I thought, could say such strange things. (Only decades and a world later did I grasp her meaning when, glimpsing into my younger daughter's golden-brown eyes, I saw the exact color of her hair.)

Liliana's short life span was to be derided by the cuckoo in one of the songs she taught us, which was making the rounds of the women's quarters:

The daughter of a shepherd was tending to her flock while, perched high on a branch, a cuckoo vocalized:
"Cookoo coo-ookoo, cookoo coo-ookoo" relentlessly the bird would call.
"Cuckoo, won't you tell the lass how many years she's meant to live?"
"Cookoo coo-ookoo," the girl was keeping track.
"Cookoo coo-ookoo, cookoo coo-ookoo" the bird went on and on.
Well past a hundred did she count: the cuckoo would not pause. The shepherdess then, angered, did shoo the bird away.

In folk tradition, the cuckoo is the foreteller of fortune and longevity. For Liliana, the cuckoo should have stopped at fifteen.

Sandu, Liliana's brother, was very handsome and just as attractive as Tudor, only older. At seventeen, he was always searching for food. The women observed that teenagers were typically ravenous at that age. His parents would collect the fat off one of the soups in our regimen and give it to him on a slice of bread between meals.

Sandu's passion was chess. They said he could play without a chessboard, in his mind, memorizing all the moves and calling them by letters and numbers. But Sandu played in our quarters with real pieces on a real chessboard, so we were able to follow his moves. By then we had reached the time in our detention when beds were brought in, and even chairs and tables, perhaps as an antidote to the fights that were erupting daily in the men's quarters. There, many games were played simultaneously, in a row of tables. After months of inaction, the activity seemed almost feverish.

Sandu, though, would play not in the men's quarters, but in the women's. He would sit at a table, the chessboard between him and another man. For hours on end I would watch him, his back slightly hunched over the table, lost in concentration, looking so handsome and smart. I started distinguishing the different pieces and their special moves. As I watched their game, I would draw closer to them and, like the fox in the *Little Prince*, I felt tamed enough until one day, with a quickened heartbeat, I dared place my hand on Sandu's shoulder. He was wearing a red-checkered shirt and a dark, knit vest. He glanced at me over his shoulder with his soft expression, then went back to playing while I, my heart still beating fast, felt bold enough to keep my hand on his shoulder.

Eventually, gentle and patient like his sister, Sandu did not mind teaching us young ones how to play the game, even though he was an expert at it. That summer, when we were allowed to go into town and sell jewelry for food, Sandu's request was not for edibles but for a chess magazine! I was in awe of him.

How to Get a Cat Drunk

Those were the days when the rules loosened up and the men who had families were allowed out. My father collected the jewels we were wearing to sell them, including the ring I had excitedly received for my sixth birthday and with which I parted without any trace of regret: the only thing that mattered now was freedom. Were we ever going to be free?

A group of fathers departed, escorted by guards. They took in the last recommendations: ". . . bring sugar . . . and don't forget alcohol!" Sugar was considered good nutrition for the children in those days, and alcohol, taken internally, a strengthening antibiotic. My father returned with these as well as meat, eggs, milk, and potatoes, which suddenly and dramatically enriched our usual daily regimen of a piece of bread and a bowl of barley or pea soup, as had also been the case in Kovačica.

For me, cooking an egg on top of boiled potatoes in a soup bowl on the room's stove was an unequaled highlight of our detention. For the women, it probably was getting the cat drunk: in an unusually bubbly mood, they put a few drops of alcohol in a spoon and spent a goodly amount of time following the cat, careful not to spill it, coaxing the reluctant feline into ingesting the potent drops. It was a circus as their moves were dictated by the cat's fancy, following it as enticingly as possible. They must have finally succeeded because the cat was zigzagging across the room, to the women's great amusement. What struck me, as a child, was the women's behavior and how much they must have needed this release: they acted like children!

Soon thereafter, more people were allowed to go to town, including the children, albeit escorted by guards. I remember the awe of glimpsing the outside world—the peach-colored walls of the houses glowing in the ripe sunlight, a cool breeze gently swaying the leaves on the trees. A sunlit alley led to a yard where beer was served and where men gathered, talking and laughing. My mother took my sister and me to a pastry shop. My father did not go with us. Perhaps he went on some errand, preferring, typically, to spend money on us, never on himself.

The shop had lovely little round tables made of light-colored wood and a long counter displaying pastries behind glass.

Pastries! How unearthly! The pastries, however, were for children alone. No adult was allowed to partake of them. My sister selected a pastry, I selected one, and with our two plates we went to a table where all three of us sat, but only two of us ate. Mother watched. The pastries looked beautiful, yet I don't remember their taste. I felt I could not swallow. How could I eat when mother could not? Yet I ate mine, and my sister hers, because we were hungry. Every swallow hurt. How unfathomable for parents—loving, generous, devoted—to watch their children eat while they could not. When the people in the pastry shop were not looking, we got mother to have a bite.

What a stark contrast with our experience in Italy, where food was abundant even though that country had lost the war!

A Shot in the Night

The outings in town did not last. They had turned up in our lives as an implausible interlude, one of those outlandish occurrences we accept without questioning. They ended abruptly, perhaps when a young man was shot.

It happened in the full darkness of night when we were all asleep. A shot tore into the silence, then a scream, then nothing. Just as suddenly the door slammed open. The lights were flipped on and a guard stood pointing a gun at us. I felt my heart fill with ice. The guard said something that expressed his agitation more than anything else. It was the "nice" guard, the short one who had five children, in whose eyes we had read compassion. Perhaps I did not believe he would do anything drastic to us. I grabbed my mother's hand and reassured her: "Don't worry, mom . . ." There were some questions, some searching glances, then he left.

The rumor spread that a young man (whom my parents identified later as Captain Negoescu, who worked as a cook in the kitchen) had been killed. He had tried to climb over the wire fence and had been shot. He had done what we were all doing, what kept us going: he dreamt of being free, of making it to the border with Greece or with Italy and then across it. He had thought about it, perhaps he had visualized climbing that fence as I had so often done. Its mesh had small holes but maybe his toes would fit into them. It was not that high so the cutting sensation on one's toes and fingers would be bearable.

But then the guards were up there, watching. Escape was all a matter of timing, of catching a moment when he was out of the sight of both guards. Maybe he had discussed his escape with friends, as I had with the boys so many times. Maybe he took some blind chance and now it was all over for him. He was dead.

The kind guard was back on duty. But not for long. Later we heard that he had been jailed himself. The feeling was that one too many detainees had tried to escape during his watch and that the officials had cracked down on him. His fate hurt us all the more because he was taken from his family and his five children. We felt that because he was not one of us, because he was from the other side of the fence, he was not supposed to share our fate. And yet, because he was compassionate, he ended up on our "side," leaving five young children behind.

Stricter Regimen

The rules became stricter after the attempted and failed escape. No more outings in town, no more pencils and paper for the adults, no more card games. And no more going to the outhouse at night. Instead, a huge barrel was brought inside, set by the door. As the night went on, it filled up, like the barrel in the movie *Dr. Zhivago*.[16] I dearly hoped I would not need it, but I did. (As I remember it now, it seemed huge, almost as tall as I was. But it could not have been because, on tip toes, I could reach the edge to empty my bladder—or maybe I climbed on something to reach the edge.)

In the morning, the door would be unlocked and the guards would wave us out: "*Aidanapoli!*" To our Romanian ears, this sounded like "Let's go to Naples!" Our hearts would shrink. The adults would snicker, "Sure, we'd love to go to Naples."

Dreams of Italy

Naples . . . Italy! Visions of Lago Maggiore suddenly swirled in my mind, evoking the trip we had taken two years earlier. A world ago. I was rowing on the lake, floating on the eerily transparent water that at

---

[16]*Doctor Zhivago* is the 1965 British film based on the 1957 novel of the same name by Boris Pasternak, who received the Nobel Prize for Literature in 1958 (which he later was forced by the Soviet authorities to decline).

once arouses thirst and quenches it, suspended several stories high above the pebble-covered sand we could see as distinctly as if there were no water at all. My stomach tickled with a mixture of fright and delight. I did not dare look below for more than a mesmerizing and disquieting glimpse: could invisible water really hold our weight?

Not far away, above the blueness of the lake, rose the most beautiful of the lake's three islands, the so aptly named Isola Bella (Beautiful Island), all tones of green and peach and orange, and, close to the horizon, the jagged mountains of Switzerland.

A ride on the funicular to the top of Mount Mottarone unveiled another glimpse of this jewel-like setting. By the window, a young mother was shyly nursing her baby, embarrassed by the loud attention of a group of merry young men.

A paradise lost.

Did that part of the world still exist now, I wondered? Could people really live there, go about their business, walk the streets as they please, repair to their homes at night? And if so, did they not explode with the exhilaration of being free?

A Stay at the Hospital, and the Promise of a Dandelion

Stories and rumors, sometimes disquieting, trickled from the men's quarters. A man was said to have been poisoned by a copper coin that had turned green. Was the man really sick or was it a ploy to leave the compound? But he was not the one taken to the hospital. Instead, I was.

It happened when I became nauseous, feverish, and my side hurt. I was taken to town for medical consultation. A cart drove me and my parents to the cheerful, white little building with a barren field in front of it that was the city's hospital. As we walked across the field, an amazing sight struck me: a lone dandelion had grown in the midst of the dirt, its perfect down crown fully opened. The dandelion was an uncanny whiff of freedom since its seeds could fly away, borne by the wind, wherever its waves would carry it, as we absolutely could not. I held my breath, for I did not want the seeds to blow away, not yet, not while they held the promise of taking off, rising above our heads toward the wide-open spaces of countries without borders, toward the free lands of our longing, toward release.

(I felt almost stabbed years later when, unexpectedly, I glimpsed an image in a French Larousse dictionary: a woman blowing on dandelion seeds, with the motto *Je sème a tout vent* (I sow to all winds). It filled me again with that feeling of existing without really living, of being invisible to the outside world, transparent like a ghost that wanders among the living while the living know not it exists.)

Past the dandelion, inside the building, a spotless, welcoming world of white beds and sheets, well-lit rooms, bright windows, and re-assuring smiles welcomed us. One of the beds was assigned to me, with its clean, crisp sheets. My mother, who was allowed to accompany me inside (but without my father), sat on a chair beside me. This is where she slept the first night, her head resting on the foot of my bed. But every time I opened my eyes, she was awake, looking very sad and worried. The doctors were caring and kind, they talked to mother in French or German, and inquired about our situation.

This is where I was given my first real meal since captivity, served on a plate with a fork—a far cry from the spoon and bowl of soup that had been our mainstay for so many months. On the plate, there was meat. Meat! I started eating, hungrily, when my mother asked: "Would you like to share a piece of your meat with your father?"

No, no, no, my whole being cried, no, it pleaded, no, I was so hungry, no!

"Yes, mother," I answered.

Like a stray, hungry dog, my father was pacing outside, back and forth, below the window next to my bed, waiting. Mother opened the window and bent over to hand him the piece of meat. My heart sank at his sight. I felt torn with pity and guilt, guilt for resenting the loss of food, guilt for begrudging him that bite of meat, guilt for not having opened my heart to him right away. I was inside, cozy and well fed, and he waited outside, looking like a starved, beaten animal.

The children in the spacious ward were up and about. They flocked around a specific nurse like butterflies to light. Her voice was melodious and soft, her manner gentle and inviting, and her green eyes held a magnetic luminosity we could not resist. She would sit on a white chair in the middle of the room, and tell us stories, and we stayed put around her as if stuck to honey. All I wanted was to look at her and listen to her and perhaps—what a treat!—to see her slow, delicate, mysterious, enchanting smile.

Since she made us all so happy by her sheer presence, I could not imagine her being other than happy. Yet she had problems that weighed heavily on her, as mother found out. She was Russian, married to a Yugoslav man and torn by a new edict: everyone had to pick a country of residence and stick by it. She could either stay with her husband, renounce her Soviet citizenship and never see her homeland again, nor her parents, nor her friends; or she could return to the Soviet Union and give up her home and her husband in Yugoslavia.

This dilemma was a result of tensions in 1949 between Yugoslavia's Communist leader, Tito, who had been trained in the Soviet Union and came to power with the help of the Soviet army, and Stalin, who could not tolerate Tito's desire to create a strong economy independent of Moscow.

Even though calm and serene, as she always appeared, her dilemma tormented her. What was she to do? No one, of course, could advise her. Her predicament impressed me, and I often wondered how she resolved it.

A few days into my stay, the doctors said I had appendicitis, but that I was too weak for surgery and there was nothing else they could do for me.[17] The doctors gave me several French children's books to take back to the compound, and we promised we would return them. I greatly looked forward to reading them.

Back in our quarters in Zrenianin, the dreary drabness of the place struck me. I had forgotten—or not realized—what it really looked like. As for the books, the guards took them away. For years it weighed on me that we never returned them.

New Arrivals—Accounts of Torture

As time went by, groups of refugees from countries other than Romania were brought in, Albanians, Bulgarians, Hungarians. The Albanians' entrance created quite a stir. The men marched in with a vigorous stride, singing in rhythm at the top of their lungs a tune we recognized instantly: a Romanian patriotic song! It turned out to be the Albanian national anthem with words adapted to the melody we knew so well. We all joined in with our own words, *Pe-al nostru steag e scris unire* (Unity is written on our flag), for a rousing, if sad, welcome to our underworld.

As always among refugees, we swapped stories of escape and detention. Some recurring prison names had a particularly sinister ring to them, places of dread such as Panchevo and Ljubljana. More than these places, however, being returned to the country they had just escaped was what they feared most. Reports had it that guards from both sides of the border would shoot at the refugees who were being returned. Those who survived would be taken as prisoners by the Communist governments and tortured with a vengeance. Some attempted suicide rather than face this fate. One man who was being

---

[17] A couple of years later, in the fall of 1951, my infected appendix was to be exhibited in front of my eyes in a glass tube by a French surgeon who proudly informed me he had performed on me the latest fashion in surgery, a "bikini cut," a minuscule side cut that, when I would be older (I was 11), would allow me to wear bikinis without any visible trace of my surgery. Every culture has its specialty and its pride!

returned managed to escape but was recaptured in Yugoslavia and brought back to our camp—his hair had turned white overnight.

The Bulgarians, having had some sort of official position, passed on the information that the Romanian Communist government had turned to their government to supply men to torture prisoners back in Romania. Unable to live with this pressure or with their conscience, they had decided to escape.

There was much talk of torture at that time, torture meant to extract confessions, to admit to acts people did not commit, to give out information they did not want to impart or did not possess. Laughing as always, Neagoe, who had been transferred with us from Kovačica, bared his calves to reveal the scars left by the bites of vicious dogs that had been released on him. Fast as he ran, despite his height and long legs, he had not succeeded to escape their fangs.

They talked of beatings; of prisoners who had endured light being shined in their eyes 24 hours a day; of prisoners who were brought to the verge of drowning, their heads pressed under water, and then revived;[18] of prisoners who had been beaten unconscious, dragged by their feet down the stairs, their heads bouncing rhythmically on every step. I shrank inwardly as I tried to imagine the pain of a bouncing head.

At night I would wonder how I could put up with such torture, were it applied to me, how I could refuse to say what I did not mean to say, refuse to incriminate whom I did not want to incriminate, how I could not give in just to have the intolerable pain cease? Some prisoners recounted how the laces of their shoes were taken away so they could not commit suicide when torture was too unbearable. I knew there was no way I could resist and felt defeated even before having been tested.

Other worries kept me up as well: what would I do with my little sister if our parents were to be shot? In my mind, when people were shot, bullets would automatically lodge in their heart and they would

---

[18]What we refer to in modern days as "waterboarding."

die. But adults' hearts are higher than children's heads, and my sister and I would survive. What then? What would we do without our parents? How would I take care of my little sister? Would a Yugoslav family be kind enough to take us in? Would that mean that we would never make it to the Free World? Surprisingly to my adult mind, I never shared those fears with my parents.

(For those who think torture would not have been applied to children, my Boulder friend Florina Barbu told me she was interrogated repeatedly after school and beaten at age 11 for refusing to reveal where her father was hiding to avoid political arrest. The beatings left traces on her body she strived to hide from her ailing mother. Beaten was also another friend, Horia Blăgăilă, at the same age and for a similar reason.)

Fights in the Camp and the Great Bathe-Out

With time, isolation, and increasing tension, up to seven fights erupted each day among the several dozen men occupying the men's quarters. Among other techniques, they were said to collect lice and throw them at each other. That adults would fight among each other was disquieting enough (there was no television in those days for us to become immune to such behavior), but lice? I could barely get used to the swarm of red and black bugs that surfaced at night, crawling on the straw around us and making it difficult to lie down and sleep. But lice were said to crawl on *you*, and this gave me the creeps. The remedy was to wash thoroughly, or to dip our hair in gasoline, but of course there was neither gasoline nor water to be had, so we did not wash at all.

One momentous exception occurred in the heat of the summer, when we all walked barefoot in the yard, the children in their undies. Most of the men had stripped to their shorts—that is, all but a handful, my father being one of them. Why should these men persist in wearing long, warm, dirty, worn-out pants in this sizzling heat? "It's a matter of dignity," mother explained. "Your father must maintain his dignity." Dignity. What does dignity have to do with wearing pants? When these pants were finally cleaned in Greece, the fabric disintegrated in spots: only slime had been keeping it together!

That summer, we had a great "bathe-out," as it were.

In the women's compound, across one corner, the women tied a rope and hung a blanket (or was it Madame Sunshine's precious sheet?). This afforded some privacy for what was to ensue behind the improvised curtain: standing undressed in a tub, one at a time, the women would pour over themselves water brought in a pail in successive trips. Each woman in the room took turns behind the curtain and luxuriated in a private, individual "shower." It all seemed so chic.

When my turn came, I was to wash without the benefit of the curtain, because I was a little girl. Perhaps the curtain was flimsily attached and had to be secured by hand as well, I don't know. But I insisted; I had turned nine on the last day of May and wanted the same privacy as the adults. The women indulged my request and, very proudly, I started washing behind the curtain. Alas, as I was rinsing off, the curtain fell, revealing me in all my nakedness. A burst of laughter greeted the event.

So much for *my* "dignity"!

Burducea Fight with My Father

Throughout his detention, Father Burducea—the towering former priest-turned-Communist-official-turned-defector who had shocked us at Kovačica with his violent diatribes—continued to scold and fume, hurling insults at his wife and daughter while they let his rage roll off them without flinching. Burducea would pick fights with others as well. One day, it was my father's turn. While Burducea screamed, my father listened calmly, looking at him with a sardonic smile. That was like pouring oil on fire. Burducea exploded, said something about tearing my father's mouth, picked up the wood-cutting ax with both hands, raised it over my father's head and shouted: "I will split you in half!!"

I could not bear to see my father's skull split in half, his brain parted, his body cut up in two pieces. Terrified, I ran all the way across the yard barefoot, in my nightgown, and shut myself in the outhouse. I lifted my head toward heaven to pray but couldn't. We had been praying every evening, for days and weeks and months for more than a year, finishing invariably with a fervent prayer to be set free, yet nothing had happened. Would God do anything now? I felt that, God or no God, if Burducea wanted to kill my father, he would do it. And I had left the scene and run away.

After my heartbeats calmed down somewhat, I slowly came out into the radiant sunshine. The commandant of the camp was crossing the yard, chatting and laughing with a group of men. I wanted to call out to him, to alert him to what was happening, to seek his help, but I did not dare. Even though he was a kind man of Romanian origin, there was a barrier between prisoners and jailors that we dared not cross. Those who did, such as a woman who was said to have flirted with a guard, were despised.

Ever so carefully I coaxed my steps toward the women's compound, wandering what a split head looked like, if it would open like a box, if the brain would come out in a bath of blood, if I would find my father lying on the floor in two pieces, his innards spread around. Much as I pushed the ghastly thoughts away, I could not chase these visions. I opened the door . . . and there stood my father, whole and bloodless, quiet amidst the total silence of the room.

The danger had passed. It would not return. Not long thereafter the Burduceas left Zrenianin, taken elsewhere or released.

Bunescu Fight

Another fight smacked of comedy, though not for us, who had never been exposed to cowboys and Indians nor to any assortment of television entertainment. It was tied to a unique event. A package for my parents had arrived from the West, sent by one of my grandfather's business associates, Adolph Marcus.[19] The package was a wonder. It contained food, including hard salami and a large jar of apricot jam. I remember waiting for my parents to open the jar and let Puiu, my sister, and me savor the exquisite concoction, but discretely so that others would not be tempted by food of which they did not partake. Neither my parents, nor Father Surducan, who was so gaunt he seemed to have no flesh on him, nor his wife, touched any.

That's when the Bunescus, a querulous middle-aged couple, let out the incendiary remark: ". . . in this place where parents grow fat at the expense of their children . . ." Before I could realize what happened, both parties closed in on each other, and there was a flurry of stretched fists as well as a pair of legs furiously bicycling in the air. The legs belonged to Mrs. Bunescu, who had flung herself on the floor. Obviously, no one had any practice in physical fights, and to most onlookers it had to be hilarious, but it scared me. A man who happened into our quarters at that precise moment would recall the scene later with great amusement: As Mrs. Bunescu, lying on her back, was vigorously agitating her legs, her skirt rode up and it became obvious she was wearing no underwear!

In time, the Bunescus left camp, and tensions calmed down.

Time Collapses

With the approach of winter, the camp was emptying, little by little. Our dreams became harbingers of departures to come. When Mrs. Besi dreamt that the car in which she was riding fell into a ditch, we all knew

[19]I learned from an interview with my father in the 1980s that my grandfather had managed to discover our whereabouts. Another of his associates, an engineer whose last name was Florian, knew a colonel in the Yugoslav secret police (UDBA) and discovered our location. The colonel came to see my father and give him some money. My father, fearing being set up, refused the money. Then, before leaving, the colonel asked my father to sign a piece of paper so he could show that the contact had been made. My father refused that as well.

what it meant and rejoiced, full of hope: She and her husband, the elderly couple with whom we had escaped across the Danube, would be leaving soon! And so it happened. They did leave, while we stayed put. Thereafter, as hard as I tried to dream that I was falling into a ditch, I never quite succeeded.

The women and children who remained were moved upstairs, where our beds touched each other and formed a cozy corner that my mother, my sister, and I occupied.

By now, this was beginning to feel like “home.” “I might as well settle in,” I thought, digging into the dirt floor with a spoon to uncover the cement below and to clean up. But the dirt had hardened, too tough to penetrate and piled too deep. I soon gave up.

As time dragged on and nothing happened, I found it harder and harder to sustain the expectation of ever leaving.

Every day, as evening approached, the adults would line up in the yard, form two rows, and the guards would go down their list of names. We would all be present, of course. Once in a while, they called the names of a few people meant to leave the camp. Our hearts beat faster: where would they be taken? Will it be work, will it be the West, will it be Romania?

But they never called our name. It felt as if we had grown roots in the hardened dirt of the yard, as if we had become pillars of the place, as if they could never let us out, for we were an integral, essential part of the camp and it would collapse if we left. Our nightly “Our Father,” prayers ended with the appeal “. . . and please God, deliver us from prison.” Would I spend the rest of my life ending my prayers with that phrase? As the adult love songs that filled our time[20] evoked blue eyes like Tudor’s, I wondered also if I would ever see him again.

---

[20]See the songs at the end of this chapter.

So I started resigning myself. That's where I was, that's where I was going to live the rest of my life. Maintaining hope requires too much energy.

Time "collapsed" into a hole. There was a timelessness, a discontinuity with the outside world that intensified the feeling of sinking.

That's when my soul sank into the soil of our detention camp, pinning it to the dirt that covered the cement.

Hopelessness—De-spair

Surprisingly, there was something warm, even welcoming about giving up hope and having a home, something more "normal" about it, and I could better enjoy our games and the people around me.

Yet just as I thought I reached at last the peace of hopelessness, just then, most unexpectedly, a glimmer of hope would slip in, on its own, taking me by surprise, wreaking havoc in the precarious balance of de-spair, the negation of hope (from the Latin word for hope, *sperare*).

Such were the airplanes that would fly over our Zrenianin compound, high up above us. All heads would lift and follow their course, like sunflowers turning toward the sun. Could those pilots see our camp? Could they detect us? Were they the long-awaited Americans coming to free us?

They were not.

I started longing for war. I didn't really know what war meant. But I thought that in war we could at least fight and defend ourselves; and if we died, it would be known; and there was hope for an end to the killings. Now World War II had ended and what was there to look forward to? We could be shot at any time without being able to defend ourselves. We could be eliminated without anyone knowing it.

Boba

The past exploded in my face, most unexpectedly, decades later, when I was working in a research lab in Boulder, Colorado. A scientist came into my NOAA office to speak with my co-worker. He introduced her to me: Boba Stankov, originally from Yugoslavia. More specifically, from Zrenianin.

Zrenianin!! Bombshell!

Can anyone have truly been born and raised in that concealed, unavowed underworld, in Zrenianin?

Zrenianin, the hidden stage of our incarceration, sealed from the rest of the world, the name that shocked me to my roots when I first saw it on a map, as if I had become privy to a most shameful act, catching someone in his most private moments, could Zrenianin have truly produced a child who grew up on the "outside," a normal childhood, while we were secreted away?

I listened to Boba in utter fascination as she told us about her beautiful city, about the economic stability following the initial political turmoil, about the shrewdness of Tito, about her dissident cousin who feared incarceration as a political prisoner and broke into a store to be classified instead as a common criminal in the hope of better treatment. Upon his release seven years later, he never mentioned prison nor politics. Only through conversations with a Yugoslavian theatrical group that came later to New York did Boba acquire an inkling of what her cousin must have experienced.

I could not bring myself to tell Boba I had been incarcerated in Zrenianin. She was so warm and open and friendly. The occasion might arise later.

In time, a professional friendship developed between us.

Christmas in Zrenianin

Another Christmas came and passed for us. This time I knew better than to hope for a pine tree, a toy cart, or extra food. No green blanket hanging anywhere, but much more sparkle and light in the air. Perhaps it was Mr. Economu's rich, vibrant voice leading us in song to the words "*Libertate, libertate, te aştept cu atâta dor,*" ("Liberty, liberty, I await you with such longing"), adapted to a familiar Romanian tune, *Ţărăncuţă, ţărăncuţă.* We all poured our hearts into that song, hoping that the year 1950 would bring some welcome change.

A Tear in Time

We were sound asleep, when suddenly the lights were turned on, jolting us awake in what felt like deep night. The guards were standing in the middle of the room, holding their perennial lists. They started reading names, as they always did—the names of those meant to leave the compound, other names, never ours, of course. I barely distinguished those names, still half-asleep. And then . . . did I hear right? "Popa. . . ."

Popa! That was our name. *Popa*! They read our name!! That had never, ever happened before. I could not believe it.

Hearing our name was shattering. It felt like a fold in time, a discontinuity. A tiny hole through which we slipped into another space. Even though I now know that our incarceration was limited in duration and I can estimate how long we were held there, a tear in my notion of time occurred and I feel we stayed there forever. Something broke inside me. I had exhausted my hoping energy, my waiting reserves. I had reached the bottom. I was there to stay. Forever.

And now, they had called our name!

Numbed by the shock, I got up and we gathered our few belongings into the backpacks with which we had escaped Romania so long ago and followed the guards, together with another group of detainees, to a large room downstairs. There, we were searched.

I remember these as tense moments, perhaps because of my father's notebook. My father had a little notebook in which he had recorded the names of people who had been detained at Kovačica and Zrenianin. But we were not allowed to have paper with us. No record of our existence.

The Yugoslav guards did not find the notebook.

Then we were led out into the night.

Songs We Sang in Incarceration

Children's Songs[21]

Kitty, Kitty

Pisicuţă pis, pis, pis,
Te-am visat azi noapte'n vis
Te spălam, te pieptenam
Fundă roşie îţi puneam . . .
Dar tu tot te-ai supărat
Şi pe mine m-ai zgâriat!

Kitty, kitty, little kitten
Last night in a dream I saw you.
Your fur I was washing well
And with ribbons I adorned it.
Still you got upset at me
And my hand you scratched!

In the Sunlight, Kitty Lounges

Pisicuţa stă la soare
Şi se linge pe picioare
Dă din cap, din ochi clipeşte
Şi mustaţa-şi netezeşte
Miau, miau, miau, miau,
Eu în casă nu mai stau
Miau!

In the sunlight kitty lounges
Licks her paws and nods her
head,
And while winking smoothes her
whiskers.
Meow, meow, meow, meow,
I'll no longer stay inside.
Meow!"

[21]Taught to us by a kindergarten teacher detained with us.

Love Songs

I Have Longed for Two Blue Eyes

Am iubit doi ochi albaştri
Şi-i iubesc poate şi-acum
Dar aseară vazui alţi
Mai frumoşi, mai nu ştiu cum.

Erau mari, adânci şi negri
Şi frumoşi din cale-afar
Cu-o privire ce te'ndeamnă
Să-i iubeşti şi-apoi să mori!

I have longed for two blue eyes.
And may love them to this day.
But last night I saw two others,
More attractive, . . . how shall I
say?

They were large, so deep and
dark,
Eyes seductive beyond words,
With a gaze that does compel
you
To adore them and then die.

The Hermit from the Ancient Abbey

Călugarul din vechiul schit
La el o zi m'a găzduit
Şi de-ale lumii mi-vorbit,
Şi de amor şi de iubit.

....

Călugarul din vechiul schit
Peste puţin a şi murit
Şi la mormânt printre sihaştrii
Plângeau amar doi ochi albaşti.

The hermit from the ancient abbey
Hosted me in his own cell,
And spoke of worldly matters,
Of longing and of love.

....

The hermit from the ancient
abbey,
Soon thereafter passed away,
And at his tomb among the
hermits,
Two blue eyes cried bitterly.

On a Path against a Tree

Pe cărare sub un brad, zău, zău, Şade un voinic supărat, zău, zău, zău "Ce stai bade supărat, zău, zău, Ori aştepţi un sărutat, zău, zău, zău"	On a path against a tree Leaned a youth with saddened mien. "Why are you disheartened, lad? Are you waiting for a kiss?"
"Cum să nu fiu supărat, zău, zău, De vestea ce am aflat, zău, zău, zău Că mândra s'a măritat, zău, zău, Cât am fost înstrăinat, zău, zău, zău"	"How could I not be upset, By the news I did just get That my girl indeed has married While I was away."
"Umblă bade'ncetinel, zău, zău, Dorul n'ai să scapi de el, zău, zău, zău Căci dragostea n'are leac, zău, zău, Decât ochii care-ţi plac, zău, zău, zău."	"Wander slowly on your path, Your longing won't fade away, For love has no other cure Than the eyes that caught your heart."

6
Escaping Execution in Macedonia

From the camp at Zrenianin, in the darkness of night, we were taken to a railroad station where we boarded a train. The adults searched for space to lie down to sleep on the wooden benches. My sister and I were hoisted onto the racks above, but the narrow bars pressed on my ribs and I could not sleep.

With daylight, we arrived at what we were told was Belgrade, Yugoslavia's capital, and were transferred to a prison with very small, barren cells. Only scratched names and dates on the dirt walls hinted at any previous human presence. Name, year. Name, year. Name, year. There was something ominous about the silence of these voices struggling to be heard.

Rumors circulated about the presence of the Red Cross in town. My mother spoke of getting in touch with them and letting them know of our existence. However, we were taken (again by train) to a mountainous region associated with the name Bitola. It was almost dark when the train stopped. Hungarians and Romanians were herded off the train together, to be separated later into two groups each assigned to a different location. Ahead of me walked a newlywed young Hungarian couple, both tall and slender, dressed alike in khaki-colored pants and jackets. (In later years, the image of Grace Kelly would conjure up for me the young woman's gentle profile and blond hair. I remember them clearly because they were fated to be killed.)

In the large hall of a one-story building where we settled on the floor, adults dug into their backpacks for saved scraps of food. My father's contained some bread and shortening. My sister and I ate hungrily while the guards laid down the law: "This is a working farm; the mountains in the distance are in Greece, fifteen kilometers [about 9 miles] away. You're allowed to go outside, but should you wander more than two kilometers [about 1.5 miles] away, you will be shot."

The next morning, sunshine flooded the little room where we and several other families had been assigned to sleep. The glory of the gleaming snow atop mountains that rose toward immaculate skies startled our eyes. The peaks in Greece seemed but a stone's throw away. Greece . . . freedom, so tantalizing, so close. My God, so close yet so far away.

Macedonia, at that time Yugoslavia's border province with Greece, was where we had landed. A vivifying whiff of spring thaw enveloped our captive lives. No more walls, no more bars, no more fences, no more guards pacing up and down with guns slung over their shoulders. Even though we were still confined by the previous evening's warning, we could stretch our gaze across the limitless distance.

In the mild January weather, I ran barefoot on dry grass with Vladimir. Vladimir was an eleven-year-old Romanian boy who, like me, had a little sister.[22] His family had escaped from Bessarabia, the Romanian province Stalin annexed to the Soviet Union and renamed the Republic of Moldova.

We ran toward a shallow stream that flowed at the base of a hill, picking up and feeling pebbles in our hands, all so unreal after the arid soil of the prison camp we had left. As we stared at the undulating hills,

---

[22]Years later, I learned that his father was an engineer named Vladimir Nocevan.

suddenly in the distance the silhouette of a dog took shape. A dog to play with! We started climbing the hill for a closer look, when a stern adult warning stopped us short: "That's not a dog. It's a wolf! Stay away!"

Sandu Economu was also exploring, but with a very different and specific aim in mind. The Economus—Sandu, Liliana, and their parents—had been brought to Macedonia with our same lot, increasing the number of refugees at the farm to several dozen. Our three families, Sandu's, Vladimir's, and my own, shared one room, and I slept next to Sandu on the straw-covered floor. The straw was prone to fires, so the fathers took turns watching the improvised heating can each night, all night. When the early sun rays awakened me before they reached Sandu's face, I would study his profile, keeping very still while he was still sleeping, intimidated by my good fortune. He was so close and so handsome.

For us younger children, 17-year-old Sandu was impressive and alluring. My contact with Sandu here, unlike at Zrenianin, was now minimal. No more chess games. While we youngsters were enjoying our newfound ability to explore the outdoors, all Sandu could think of was Greece. He went wild. Like a bucking colt straining to break its reins, Sandu was restlessly, feverishly searching for a way to escape.

Enclosing the farm on three sides was a loop of the Crna Reka, the Black River. A bridge ensured passage to the other side—the Greek side. The bridge was patrolled day and night by armed guards. Sandu set his mind on observing the timing of the change of guards and the interval during which a swift escape would be feasible. Vladimir had become friends with Sandu and kept me updated on his ongoing plans. The river must have carried deep and treacherous waters, for there was no talk of swimming across it. Could the horses we spotted in the fields become somehow part of an escape, we wondered.

On the evening of January 31, 1950, the guards entered our room saying they were going to take some of us to Greece. To Greece! At last!

From their perennial lists, they read about two dozen names, including those of four young Hungarian women who had been transferred to our farm. But these women by then had checked into a hospital. As rumor had it, they really were not sick but acceded to the privilege of better food, beds, and linens, thanks to their friendly relationships with some of the guards.

The guards in our room seemed annoyed. Since the Hungarian women were not available for the departure, four others were to leave in their stead. But who? My father became tense and restless. He told my mother he wanted us to take the place of the four Hungarian women and leave. My mother looked up at the clothesline that stretched across the room with our woolen underwear hanging to dry. She was reluctant. "The children's underwear is still wet. I don't know. Let's not go." My father became more and more agitated. My mother remained unconvinced. We stayed.

Meanwhile, Sandu was chomping at the bit. His family should take the place of the Hungarian women. This was their chance to reach Greece! But his parents were hesitant, not knowing what to think. Sandu was pressing, arguing, pushing. In the short time available to make up their minds, he won his parents over. Some words were exchanged with the guards, and the decision was made: the four Economus would take the place of the Hungarian women.

My father was disheartened. We were possibly missing a unique chance to be free at last. The twenty-some people selected to leave gathered their scant belongings and were ready to go. The guards directed them through our room and to the window. One by one they climbed out the window into the night.

Out the window? I wondered. How strange. Why?

The last one to scale the windowsill was a young medical student my parents remembered as Teodor Grigorescu. He turned to my father and sought his advice: "Mr. Popa, what should I do? Should I go? Should I try to stay? I don't even have shoes fit for the mud outside." My father handed him a pair of shoes left by Father Voştenaru, a priest who had been returned to Romania several months back, and the young man left.

That night, after the excitement of the departure subsided, images of Greece, only 15 kilometers away, filled our dreams: oranges, sardines, olives, balmy winters.

As the morning sunshine woke us up, Greece again filled our minds. We envied the group that had left: "They are probably eating breakfast now, oranges, sardines, olives." A kind of expectant exhilaration filled us, because perhaps soon our turn would also come.

There was not much time to indulge in such fantasies, for presently there arose some sort of commotion. A man from yesterday's group was found sleeping on the straw in the barn, exhausted. Awakened, in a somber mood and none too communicative, he reluctantly recounted that, feeling uneasy about the destination of the trip and being an electrician by trade, he had followed the telephone poles back to the farm, pretending to be checking the telephone lines to escape notice. The guards seemed very irritated to find him there.

As the peasant workers arrived at the farm, they reported that they had been called during the night to bury a group of people. From their descriptions, the adults recognized last night's group. They had been killed. A spirited discussion ensued with the guards regarding this execution. The guards denied it, insisting that the group was now in Greece. When confronted with the peasants' reports, the guards finally backed down and admitted that, yes, they were killed, but that's because they tried to escape.

"But you led them away!"

> Alerted of our plight by a refugee who had escaped from the camp, in 1949 French diplomat Robert Morisset asked the Yugoslav authorities to let the refugees go and offer them *laissez passer* (free passage) into France. The response was: "What refugees? There are *no* refugees detained in Yugoslavia." Some fifty years later, in 2001, when Romanian TV producer Lucia Hossu-Longin searched for the camp where we were held in Zrenianin for her documentary series *Memorialul Durerii* on persecutions under the Communist regimes, she was told in no uncertain terms that there had been no such camp and she was threatened away.

"No, they tried to escape, and the proof is that they climbed out the window," the guards insisted. My fear—even horror—of lies must have originated then.

Vladimir and I were tremendously shaken and subdued. We talked about nothing else during the days that followed. I was wondering what it would feel like to have a bullet go through one's heart. I thought that was what being shot meant: the bullet, like a missile pulled by a magnet, would aim for the heart, would pierce it, and bingo! the person would be dead. One would have to put up with the momentary pain of the penetration, then all would be ended. In this world.

I believed in life in another world. A good, serene life with a loving God, where we would find our beloved ones like Sandu and Liliana. But I wasn't ready to die. I was curious about life, about what it was like to be an adult.

Maybe there was a way of communicating with Sandu and Liliana even if we were not killed and reunited in the other world—a way to find out what happened to them and how they felt about it, maybe by spiritism, which, as we heard the adults describe it, was calling on spirits to answer our questions by moving an overturned glass on letters spread on a table.

Sandu and Liliana's family and friends were very much on our minds. Vladimir had filled me in on Sandu's life back in Romania where he had left a girlfriend. Thoughts of Sandu's girlfriend were always present. How could we contact the Economus' loved ones and tell them what happened? The thought that they had been killed and that no one back home would know about it preoccupied me intensely. We were sunk in a hole in the underworld, totally cut off from the outside world, even though—unlike previously—that hole could now appear sunny with wide open spaces on the outside. They shot Sandu and Liliana and had the gall to deny it to us, who knew the truth. How would anyone else be able to find out about the death of our friends?

> My father eventually reported these killings, in French, to Swiss bureaucrats. As he was leaving, but still within earshot, the Swiss turned toward each other and wondered in German, a language in which my father was fluent: "This man looks reliable. Why do you think he makes up such stories?" And 51 years later, after the Iron Curtain came crashing down and Romanian television documented our escape as part of their series on Communist persecutions, *Memorialul Durerii* (Memorial of Suffering), I was put in touch with Zelma Sfetescu (Mrs. Economu's niece, the daughter of her brother), to whom I revealed their fate. She had no idea what had happened to them.

A couple of days after the killing of the Economu group, on February 2, 1950, officials came to the farm. They called my father and Vladimir's father to confer with them behind closed doors.

My mother was waiting in our room, tense, her face ashen. I did not totally comprehend her acute anxiety. All activity seemed to have come to a halt while the two fathers were in discussion with the officials. In what language, I could not figure out, since my father did not know Serbo-Croatian. (Many, many years later, as I was writing my recollections, I asked my father whether he used a mixture of Serbo-Croatian, German, Romanian, and other languages. My father said he could not remember, only that he was very forceful. Maybe this is where his intense sense of "our rights" saved him.)

One hour, two hours went by. Finally, the door opened and the fathers came out, drained. They revealed that the officials had come to "take them to Greece," just the two of them, without their families. True to his training as a lawyer, my father had argued for hours trying to dissuade them. He was certainly not willing to go without his family. Convincing the officials not to take him and Vladimir's father "to Greece" must have been one of the greatest feats of my father's existence. It saved his life.

Shortly thereafter, the officials went to the other farm, where the Hungarian group had been taken. The young Hungarian newlyweds who had walked ahead of me the night of our arrival, she in the likeness of Grace Kelly, were summoned to go "to Greece" in the place of Vladimir's father and my own. We heard that they, too, were shot and killed.

Eventually, the four hospitalized Hungarian women returned to the farm. The adults surmised they had stayed at the hospital, warned by their boyfriends, long enough to escape the fate of the Economu group.

One evening several days later, on February 8, 1950, the guards came to our room and ordered our family and some others to gather our belongings: they were taking us to Greece.

One of the guards was dark-haired and handsome, with a black mustache. He was said to be Muslim. Using sign language and a few words of Serbian, my mother asked him whether this trip would be "good" or "bad." "Good" he signaled and pointed to the watch on my mother's wrist. Mother readily handed him the watch. She reasoned that if we were to be killed, he could simply take the watch after she was dead. "This watch has not brought me good luck," she commented. She added that their religion required Muslims never to lie, so maybe he was telling the truth.

We packed our belongings in our backpacks and when we were all ready, the guards told us to go out the window, just as they had required of Sandu and Liliana's group. My father protested vehemently: if we left, it would have to be out the main door.

My child's mind could not comprehend my father's insistence. What difference would it make which way we left the farm? Who would know what happened in our underworld anyway?

In the end, we went out the main door, wide open, all thirteen of us. It was late, the darkness abated by a bright moon. Temperatures had dropped over the past few days and the mud had frozen. As we stepped over the thin layer of ice, it would break and we would sink into the mud. The American shoes I had picked from packages sent from the United States felt even tighter now.

We started walking, bundled up and huddled, into the cloudy night. Sometimes the moon shone and we could clearly see our group and the trees around us. Sometimes the clouds covered the moon, and it would be all dark. Several guards accompanied us. I remember the hilly terrain, the shots the guards fired in the dark "to keep the wolves away." Valdimir and I wondered, "When will it be the wolves and when us?"

As we continued our march, Valdimir and I pondered the good deeds we had done in our lives that perhaps would spare us from being shot. I remembered a dead bird I had found once back in Romania and had buried. Could that spare me? Vladimir recalled similar incidents and hoped those might protect him.

As we crossed an open field, the guards suddenly ordered us to lie flat on the ground and remove any white clothing we were wearing. I removed my woolen hat. Then a truck passed on a road not too far away. When it was gone, we resumed our march. The guards explained that we should not be seen. Why not?

As the hours went by, I started feeling my energy drain out of my body. My mother asked my father to stop a moment so she could find, in his back pack, a piece of sugar for me. As she struggled to unzip one of the pockets, she pulled at the backpack. My father, bristling with impatience, pulled away. I had never seen him that way when it was a matter of giving us food. He had to be very, very tired. He could no longer carry my little sister. Some of the other men carried her for a while, for as long as they could bear her weight, which was very light even for a four-year-old. Then they would set her down and she would walk on her own.

After a long time, we came upon some wet haystacks and we were allowed to sit on them and rest. But before we could unwind we had to tear ourselves away and walk again.

It was now a mountainous setting with streams along the way. My shoes were hurting badly but it was a matter of pride for Vladimir and me not to complain and keep up with the adults. I wanted to wade through the water like Vladimir and everyone else and I protested loudly when someone picked me up and carried me across to dry land. Then I realized I would have had to walk with wet shoes and socks and was secretly grateful.

As we struggled to keep the steady rhythm of our march, which made the pain of every step more bearable, suddenly, as if there was nothing better in the world to do, my little sister stopped and bent over to pick a flower! In extreme irritation, I was about to scold her for that senseless and painful break in our rhythm when my parents, to my dismay, melted at the gesture and carefully put the edelweiss away.[23] (My irritation at her gesture mellowed years later, in Paris, when my own four-year-old daughter stopped by every flower she spotted on the sidewalks and declared, in her newly acquired French: "*Moi j'aime toutes les fleurs!*" ("Me, I love all flowers!").)

My little sister, trudging along, nursing her own private fears,[24] my little sister also loved flowers, even in the muddy hills of Macedonia, even in the darkness of a night fraught with wolves and seared by the sound of gunshots, pregnant with the weight of an uncertain outcome.

---

[23]The flower still lies pressed between the pages of a now-faded book from my parents' library.

[24]She disclosed this to me forty years later.

Thus the night passed, occasionally lit by a moon that slipped in and out of the clouds, until we reached the top of a hill. The guards pointed to the valley below and directed us to go down into it. Greece was there, they said, and they left us.

I thought I misunderstood.

Suddenly the clouds parted, the moon shone brightly and the thirteen of us stood in uncertainty.

An animated discussion arose among the adults. Which way to go? Should we follow the guards' instructions? Should we take another path?

My mother, having lost her own mother at an early age, had been raised by her father, an officer in the Romanian navy. He had shared his knowledge of astronomy with her, and she was very familiar with scrutinizing the night sky on ships and could guide herself by the stars and the moon. The movement of the moon that night, she explained, indicated that South was to our left. South is where Greece was. So we should turn left.

There was a moment of heated argument among the men, but finally it died down, and we all headed left as my mother had indicated.

Day was breaking now and the surroundings were bathed in an unreal hue with vaguely defined, undulating shapes.

A worrisome gray silhouette seemed to be dancing ahead of us, but as the shape became sharper and more stable, I recognized it to be a man from our group. At that point we came upon a road—a narrow dirt road spotted with little white stones. "Marble!" my mother exclaimed. "Marble is the signature of Greece."

We turned right to follow it. The growing daylight clarified objects ahead of us. It did not take long until the outline of small houses appeared. On one of them stood out a large official insignia representing a crown.

A crown! No longer the dreaded, ubiquitous red star, Stalin's red star, the star of the Soviet Union that the head of Yugoslavia, Tito, having been trained in Moscow, had adopted for his country. Instead, it was the crown of the kingdom of Greece.

"Greece!" the adults exclaimed, "We are in Greece!"

We had made it.

At that moment, a cock crowed.

7

AHLADA AND THE ARITHMETIC OF KILLING

We had reached the border town of Ahlada, which lies between the cities of Bitola in Macedonia and Florina in Greece. After a short respite for us to feed on bread, lemon, and sardines, the Greek officials came to debrief us. The Greek translator, who knew Romanian, turned out to be—to my parents' enormous surprise—Leontis, the brother of one of my grandfather's business associates. They talked as old acquaintances would. The translator reported that about a week earlier a Romanian man had escaped from Yugoslavia and told his story. He and a group of Romanian refugees had been led by Yugoslav guards from a farm in Macedonia through the mountainous region leading to Greece. They walked into the night until they arrived at the top of a hill where the guards instructed them to continue, alone, into the valley, to reach Greece.

Following the guards' instructions, they reached the bottom of the valley, whereupon shots rang from above and all around, killing all in the group except this one man. He started running. A guard saw him and pointed his gun at him but by now the gun was unloaded. The guard raced after him, then suddenly stopped and swore; the refugee had just crossed the border into Greece.

The conclusion was inescapable. That man had just reported the fate of our friends, as well as of Teodor, the young medical student to whom my father had given a pair of shoes.[25]

> The confirmation of the execution of the Economu family is contained in a letter sent to me on March 7, 1987, by Robert Morisset, the French diplomat in Belgrade at the time. He had himself obtained the confirmation from his Athens colleague, Paul Fouchet, based on the report of the Greek border police. Upon learning of their execution, confirmed by the Greek border police, the French diplomat in Belgrade at that time, Robert Morisset, expressed his pain. He had briefly met them in Belgrade and had been particularly impressed by the quality of the parents and the striking beauty of the children. (See Appendix F.)

The arithmetic of the killings started to make sense: two people had escaped the execution of the Economu group: the refugee who made it to Greece and the electrician who had returned, unobserved, to the farm. Therefore, two other people had to be killed in their stead. The first choice was my father and Vladimir's father. Their resistance and their arguments were effective, so the young Hungarian couple was executed.

What was the rationale for these executions? The answer came, again from the Greek translator: Not much earlier a young Yugoslav guard had also defected there. He explained that refugees were killed at the border as an example for the local population who might attempt to cross over to Greece. "See this group you buried?" they would be told, "They were shot because they tried to escape." This was population control through terror, as Lenin had taught.

---

[25]About three decades later, my parents received a letter forwarded from Canada and inquiring about the fate of the young medical student. His father had written from the Romanian province of Oltenia that he had heard that his son, who had escaped in 1948 to Yugoslavia, was now a doctor and doing well, with a family of his own. He had received no news from him and did not mind if he did not write. He wanted to know only about his fate. Was what he heard true? My parents were faced with a dilemma: to tell the father the truth, or to let him keep on believing his son was alive and well. I don't know what my parents' answer was, if any.

Post Mortem Shock

Only after 68 years, spurred by the questions of a team from present-day Romania aiming to locate and inter the remains of the Economu group did I realize that we also were slated to be executed. This realization stunned me, for I had always felt that perhaps there was a chance we would be spared. But the evidence points overwhelmingly to the contrary:

In answer to the team's questions, I examined the logistics of the execution of the Economu group. To kill twenty-some people by gunshot without any of them escaping, they had to be shot all at once from all around in a reasonably enclosed space, such as a valley at the bottom of a hill. Also, for the guards not to shoot each other inadvertently, the shooters had to position themselves slightly above the group, which explains why the man who managed to run away and reach Ahlada reported hearing shots from above and all around. Finally, it had to be a sustained volley of bullets to ensure they all died, which explains why the gun of the guard who saw the man running away was unloaded soon after the shooting started.

With this set-up, it became inescapable that the following sequence of events had to lead to our execution:

1. The guards told us to climb out the window. This would allow them to claim, as they did with the Economu group, that we had attempted to escape.
2. They told us to remove anything that would make us visible. This would allow them to hide the fact that *they* led us to the border with Greece, rather than *our* attempting to reach it.
3. They told us to go down to the bottom of the hill where, they claimed, we would be in Greece. The bottom of the hill actually was where the Economu group was executed. Greece was much closer, to the left.

A question remains: Why did the guards not attempt to retrieve us once they realized we were not coming ? The answer is very simple: they could not retrieve us because, when we turned to the left instead of heading down the hill, we almost immediately entered a wooded area that camouflaged us and we came upon a short and level trail that led us very soon to the Greek village of Ahlada. We were obviously out of reach.

This illustrates how easy it was for the local population to cross over to Greece, were they not discouraged by fear. And fear is what the government aimed to instill by taking people to the Greek border and killing them, following Lenin's admonition to control populations through terror.

I was devastated by this revelation. This meant they planned to kill my little four-year-old sister who loved flowers and slowed down our laborious trek to pick one in the night. How was she going to react when she heard the shots, the screams, and she saw the adults fall down?

It meant they also planned to kill Vladimir's six-year-old sister along with us all. As hard as I tried, I could not grasp this reality—that they were going to kill little children, even though I knew they had killed the Packers, a young couple and their baby.

One never hears of Greeks or Italians killing families with young children who reach their shores, especially not after detaining them for a year or more, even though they are overwhelmed by the influx of refugees. Why did the government of neighboring Yugoslavia choose to follow the Soviet example and Lenin's teachings?

The present realization that I should have been dead for 68 years as well as the horror of the haphazard method of execution shake me to the depth of my core. But I am intensely aware that I have been blessed with a long and rich life, including becoming a mother and grand-mother, and I am filled with profound gratitude for my mother's initiative and Heaven's protection.

My twin grandchildren, Adrian and Alina, with their mother Domnica and me. Photo by my daughter Adriana.

A New Destination

We were walking again now, toward a new destination. The word "camp" reached my ears and panic struck. "Camp" is what they called Zrenianin. A wave of despair surged from the depth of my being. To my utter surprise, I thought I would rather die than relive what we had gone through. Had incarceration really weighed on me so crushingly that I would rather die than repeat that experience? (This was the first indication that I had been shaken to my roots, much more than I allowed myself to believe, and this trauma would strike me decades later.)

Our detention experience, however, was not repeated. A "camp" in Greece turned out to be worlds apart from a "camp" in Yugoslavia, even though these were two neighboring countries. The camp at

Lavrion, Greece, welcomed us with open doors and windows and clean beds with sheets. We could go out and wander about the streets as free as birds. Our meals consisted of large, satisfying bowls of delicious noodles sprinkled with sugar. I had to ingest them carefully, though, because at first my stomach could not assimilate such rich food and made me nauseous.

The next stop was Athens. My father managed to communicate with Mr. Besi, with whom we had escaped across the Danube into Yugoslavia, who agreed to be a guarantor for us. A truck dropped us off at a hotel in Omonia Square and left us there—no longer led, escorted, or followed by anyone. A very strange feeling:

We were *FREE!*

Wandering about the sunny streets of Athens, past tables laden with mountains of oranges, past endless expressions such as *efharistopoli* (thank you) and *separacalopoli* (please), shaking off the ghosts of past confinement, I felt tormented by the need to express what we had endured. How could I impart the despair of a situation still ongoing for those we left behind? I felt deep frustration at my total inability to wield words. But I was not yet ten and writing would have to wait until I went to school again.

Athens – Paris – New York, and a New Beginning

Greece is very close to Romania geographically as well as historically (the Romanian harbor of Constanţa on the Black Sea is the ancient Greek port of Tomis dating from antiquity); culturally (many schools in the Romanian provinces were run by Greeks in past centuries); religiously (both countries are Christian Orthodox); and affectively, since so many of us count Greeks among our friends and our ancestry. (Elisa Iatropol, my great-grandmother, hails from a Greek family established in Romania.)

In Athens, where my grandfather knew a huge number of people, Greek friends and acquaintances, some being refugees themselves, came as in a pilgrimage, to greet "the son of Apostol Popa." They helped in whatever way they could with their limited resources. Mr. Besi lent us money with which my parents bought us—a luxury!—nightgowns, sandals, coats.

But the problem for my parents now was where to find jobs.

Greece was flooded with refugees, this time from Soviet-controlled countries. Huge posters hanging from the ceiling of the refugee center depicted radiant scenery from Australia and New Zealand, meant to lure us to those faraway lands. But that was before air travel, and those destinations struck us like moving to the moon, never to return.

The French consul in Athens granted us entry visas in France, with passage through Switzerland, thanks mainly to three benefactors: French diplomat Robert Morisset in Belgrade, who had been made aware of our existence by other refugees; Mr. Parisot, the French military attaché in Bucharest; and Father Chorung, a French priest who knew our family well.

In post-war France, however, despite my mother's French education at the Notre Dame de Sion convent in Galați, despite my father's Doctorate in Law from the Sorbonne in Paris, despite their spur-of-the-moment training as a book binder (my father) and a beautician (my mother), they could find no employment.

While searching for a solution, mail from Romania reached us through friends. We heard that after our escape, my grandfather back in Romania had been taken to the police station and interrogated: "Where is your son?" His exclamation: "I would give anything to know where he is" earned his release. I was bursting with longing to tell him how much I missed him, but all we could safely write were innocuous daily occurrences under assumed names.

My Uncle Horia was in prison. His wife, Aunt Helga, had to hide the fact that she was the wife of a political prisoner in order to fend for herself and her two small sons. Another uncle, Constantin Niculescu, denounced for a careless political joke during a bridge game, was sent to the notorious Aiud prison where he would spend five years. Each prison had a certain resonance, simply from the tone of voice, the expression on people's faces when they pronounced the name: Aiud was one of the worst.

Mail brought me a note from Tudor, folded over a dried edelweiss: *Din Munţii Bucegi, găsită de mine, pentru ziua ta, dragă Grid* (From the Bucegi Mountains, found by me for your birthday, dear Grid). My tenth birthday had occurred at the end of May. Tudor's message must have meant the world for me. (I can still read it in my mind's eye, but I recall no joy.) Numb is how I felt, as if my heart were dead: what should the note mean, since it was too dangerous to write to him, since we were worlds apart and all the bridges over the abyss that separated us had been severed?

Like patients freshly out of the hospital after major surgery, we were drained of energy, weak and lost in the stream of life that flowed vigorously around us while we had to find the emotional strength to seek a new place in the world. We needed to convalesce. We started with a stay at the village of Les Rousses, in the French Jura mountains, in the summer of 1950. While I was looking at a book for children explaining how grape juice was made into wine, I caught a glimpse of my mother holding a letter in her hand. Her face started contorting and tears glistened in her eyes: she was informed that her younger sister, my Aunt Lydia, had been arrested.[26]

Back in Paris, a bomb exploded in the Communist Party headquarters. I burst with elation: could this be the beginning of the end?

---

[26]Aunt Lydia was to spend the next four years at the Mislea penitentiary for women for having harbored a priest at a time when priests were persecuted by the Communist government. She was condemned for "counter-revolutionary activity." Appendix C presents a copy of her criminal record.

Our family in Switzerland after our escape from Yugoslavia, 1950.

Will the Soviet troops be expelled from Romania? Will things finally return to normal?

No. We had to seek a new normal, and for me it became the public elementary school on the Rue de la Ville-l'Évêque. I was enrolled in *huitième* (literally, eighth grade, but in the French system students start in the eleventh grade and count grades backward). My classmates were girls younger than I was because I had to start making up for the years of schooling I had lost.

The French language presented an extra challenge to me, but an energizing one. In math, exhilarated, I solved 3, 4, 5 extra problems while the rest of the class was just finishing our assigned work. A touching moment occurred in *écriture* (handwriting practice) when the word selected by our teacher, Madame Fournier, was "*Bucarest*" (the French spelling for Bucharest)! My heart leapt with joy. She knew that was my hometown. She acknowledged my world and made it easier for me to become a part of her world.

But we were destined not to stay in France—there were no jobs and we lived on borrowed money. We needed to move on.

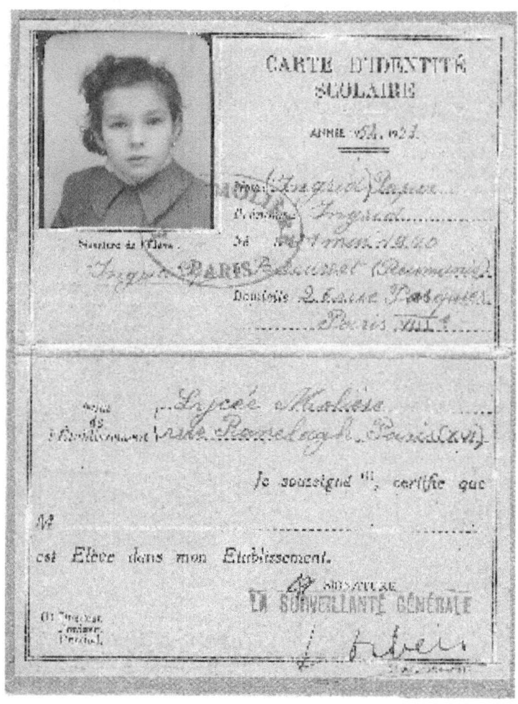
CARTE D'IDENTITÉ
SCOLAIRE

Signature de l'Élève

Domicile

Lycée Molière

Je soussigné, certifie que

M

est Élève dans mon Établissement.

LA SURVEILLANTE GÉNÉRALE

My French school identity card for 1952–1953; instead, I attended school in the United States.

After skipping a grade to make up for lost time in Yugoslavia, seven months into my sixth grade at the Lycée Molière (which corresponds to the sixth grade in the United States), we prepared to cross the Atlantic to the New World. The United States was open to refugees within the limits of a quota system.[27] The countries relegated behind the Iron Curtain had their borders sealed, so very few were those who succeeded in escaping, and the Romanian quota was still open.

The move to the faraway American continent was made easier by the nightmarish fear of the Soviet troops, which had advanced as far west as Austria, a mere 100 miles from the Eastern border of France in the Jura, where we had vacationed.

Rebirth and new roots were to emerge eventually in the United States after a decades-long and emotionally harrowing struggle to adjust to the lopsided world that emerged from World War II in the ominous shadow of the Soviet Union.

On April 19, 1952, my father, my mother, my sister, and I boarded the ocean liner *Ile de France* and we were on our way to New York.

[27]According to the Immigration Act of 1924.

8

UNDERTOW IN NEW YORK: THE SOVIET GRIP ON THE UNITED STATES

I . . . wanted all English-speaking people and everyone in the West to know about the inhumanity of the Soviets and their hirelings. I was hoping that the reaction of the free nations would lead to help for all those in the camps and the prisons in the Soviet Union.

The Long Walk[28]
Gulag survivor Slawomir Rawicz
Lyons Press, Guilford, CT 2010

I yearned for such a reaction too.

Arrival in the United States

On April 26, 1952, via the transatlantic liner *Ile de France*, we landed on American soil. New York lay ahead: crowds overflowing into the

[28]This book inspired Peter Weir's film, *The Way Back* (2010).

streets and intermingling with bumper-to-bumper traffic; chewing gum dispensers amazingly activated by a penny, and turnstiles activated by a nickel in every subway station; Nestle Quik mixed with milk and ice cubes warded off the intense summer heat (air conditioning was scarce in those days); and timid forays into English learned from TV Westerns. I gleefully attempted to emulate the Wild West among the rocks in Central Park with the Teodoru twins, wearing my twelfth-birthday gift of a cowboy outfit (no cowgirl skirts to be found). Dan and Doru Teodoru had crossed the Atlantic with us. There was something inherently dynamic and regenerating on this continent, a time of stimulation and amazement.

My parents registered me and my sister at the French Lycée on 95th Street in Manhattan to continue our studies after our two years of schooling in France. No one from Romania believed the travesty of the rigged elections (now notorious in the annals of fraudulent elections) that brought the Communists to power in our homeland with an unheard-of 80 percent of the vote. Thinking this government could last no more than a few years, we expected to return home soon. My mother was hired as an aide at the Lycée, then as a math teacher. My father, who could not put to use in the United States his French degree in Roman Law, earned a master's degree in accounting from Columbia University. Based on his experience in the textile industry in Romania, he then was hired as a financial officer at Reliance Manufacturing Company, a prominent textile manufacturer[29] for which he eventually became the treasurer.

I attended school with enthusiasm. My thirst for knowledge manifested in avidly studying every subject: Latin, French, German, English, science, math, history, geography, literature. I felt like a sponge, eager to soak up everything there was to know. And I meant to

---

[29]See "Safie Brothers Wins Control of Reliance Co." (*Chicago Daily Tribune*, August 30, 1955, Sports/Business section, pp. 7–8).

use it all to assist in rebuilding Romania, to help her heal her wounds and start anew.

On the surface lay the immense joy of going to school, of diving into the brilliant world of foreign cultures, of wondrous travels to Western Europe to be closer to Romania but without ever being able to reach it. However, beneath the excitement of our new life in a new world lay the undertow of the reality we left behind and the dramatic changes after World War II.

In France, I had heard comments on my "lovely accent, just like Elvire Popesco's"[30] or echoes of actors and writers of Romanian origin, famous in France at that time: Alice Cocea, Yonnel, Marthe Bibesco. A world of Romanian connections from before the war that no longer existed. In Italy, strangers in train stations would recall with pleasure such and such contact with Romanians "before the war," their trips to Romania "before the war." I heard about Romania's participation in the 1939 Paris and New York World's Fairs, in international competitions of wines, of poetry—all before the war.

Now, in New York, Romania seemed almost nonexistent. No Romanian books, no Romanian community with whom to speak our native tongue except on Sundays at St. Dumitru's Romanian Orthodox Church on 89th Street in Manhattan, no awareness of Romanian history, culture, jokes. Never in the news, never on the international scene. Once my heart almost stopped when I heard on the radio the Romanian song "*Ciocârlia*" ("The Lark"), which was ingrained in me like my very breath. It was presented as a Soviet song from the Soviet Republic of Moldova, which had been the Romanian province of Bessarabia until the Molotov–Ribbentrop Act of August 23, 1939. By this act, Hitler and Stalin secretly agreed to "spheres of influence" in Europe. Stalin annexed the Romanian province of Bessarabia and

---

[30]A very popular actress who cultivated her much-appreciated Romanian accent in French.

renamed it the Moldavian Soviet Socialist Republic or Moldova, even though that name belonged to a province already existing in Romania. (In Romanian, the name of the Romanian province and of the Soviet Republic are identical.) Having taken one of our provinces and erased its name, the Soviets now claimed as their own our songs, our soul. Romania was engulfed in the Soviet abyss.

A pall of death settled on our former existence. There were so few of us who had managed to escape. I felt the whole burden of speaking up, of "letting the world know we still existed," weighed on my shoulders. (I felt I was sinking," my future husband, Mircea, would relate later about his own emotions in this period.)

Yet Romania, with our friends, with my aunts, uncles, and grandparents, did exist, even if in a dark limbo. Once in a great while news about them would trickle out and reach us, in tortuous paths, through rumors passed on by others or letters received for us by the superintendent of our building under an assumed name ("Mureşan" c/o superintendent). Because of our escape, our family in Romania was under surveillance by the secret police. My mother would dictate to me letters to her sister so the censors, who regularly opened letters, would not recognize her handwriting.

If this seems like a far-fetched precaution, consider that after the 1989 collapse of the Communist regime, my husband discovered in his files at the Securitate (Romania's secret police) photocopies of letters his brother had sent him in California, photocopies of letters my husband had written to his mother in Romania, photographs of him and his friends at graduate school in Berkeley. Even retrospectively, it was a creepy invasion of our private lives.

All along, under assumed names, we were sending parcels to our families to help them in their misery when food was scarce in a formerly rich country that had attracted so many of my ancestors—Austrian, Greek, Scottish, German, Croatian, all who came to that land for a better living. Underwear was a rarity that could be obtained through Yugoslav channels, as we learned later from friends. Medicine and antibiotics were sometimes nonexistent. Only through connections could Father Gâldău, now the priest at St. Dumitru's Church in New York, succeed in sending, via the diplomatic pouch, an antibiotic that saved his son's life back in Romania.

In this atmosphere of uncertainty and dread, news reached us that Romanian girls were being deported from Bessarabia (again, renamed the Republic of Moldova) to underpopulated, remote areas of the Soviet Union as part of the Soviet policy to reshape the ethnic composition of its empire, the better to control it.[31] Echoes of these mass deportations surfaced at the Eurovision Song Contest 2016 with the winning entry, "1944," composed and performed by a Ukrainian Tatar in recollection of the 1944 deportation by Stalin of Crimean Tatars that included her great-grandmother. Such deportations felt threatening to our collective identity. I could accept my individual death. Others would take my place. But if our entire nation, our history, our culture disappeared in a collective death, what would be left of who we, and the generations who preceded us, had ever been?

In reaction to the threat of losing our identity, having learned dances from Stu Lipner, an American folk dancing enthusiast, I organized a Romanian folk dance group in New York. It eventually appeared on a TV Christmas show and was performed in 1964 at the New York State Pavilion of the New York World's Fair. It was a statement to the world: Look, we still exist, we have folk music, a language, and art that enrich the world just as others do—we have not been totally eradicated. "You act as if these dances were a matter of life and death," exclaimed one of the dancers as I pressed them to train for a performance in Central Park. It was indeed a matter of life and death for me and much more

[31]See *The A to Z of Moldova* by Andrei Brezianu and Vlad Spânu (Scarecrow Press, Lanham, MD, 2010) about deportations from Romania.

than my own death. For in those days, Romania seemed to have disappeared from the map.

The Hungarian Revolution

Suddenly, in 1956, an unbelievable event shook our world.

The slowly surging tide of discontent and the yearning for liberty in East Germany and in Poland suddenly exploded in Hungary. In October, students in the thousands came out in the streets of Budapest, demanding freedom and independence from Moscow, facing the Soviet tanks with flags alone. The Hungarian troops joined them.

Was this the answer to my fervent prayers for our liberation at the pilgrimage town of Lourdes, in France, before sailing for the United States? Amidst the mobs of the faithful, the multitude of candles, the religious souvenirs, the names carved into the wall's massive blocks of stone in gratitude for miraculous healings, I had prayed for Romania's liberation.

But reinforcements then began pouring in from the Soviet Union through Romania, "spreading death and destruction" according to the news reports. In Bucharest, thousands of students demonstrated against the Soviet Union and in support of the Hungarians. I wondered, what are Tudor and Anca doing?

(Tudor, as I found out 45 years later in a May 1, 2015, telephone conversation with Anca, was actively organizing student demonstrations in University Square in Bucharest, asking for freedom and chanting, "Long live the Hungarians! Down with the Soviets!" Two of his friends were arrested. Under police interrogation, they refused to name Tudor as one of the demonstrators, thus saving him. One of his friends was savagely beaten, the other was exiled in the province and only 20 years later allowed to return to Bucharest to finish his degree in architecture. Upon their release, both were pressured to cooperate with the Securitate by reporting their friends' actions and behavior.)

The governments of the United States, France, and Great Britain were absorbed by the Suez Canal crisis and the budding war in that region. Radio Free Europe encouraged the young Hungarians to keep up the fight, but no concrete US government support followed. I was sixteen and yearning to join in the battle against the Soviet troops. But I did not know Hungarian and I wasn't sure I had the courage to die in a foreign country and inflict this pain on my parents. Would my death be useful? I felt I would readily have exchanged my life for the liberation of Romania. But does such an exchange really exist? Which is harder, to die while fighting or to fight while living?

Churning inside with idle, frustrated energy, living in my mind with the rebels, hammering into the piano the chords of Chopin's revolutionary etude inspired by another Russian invasion, practicing my fencing lunges on *Life* magazine's photograph of a seemingly bloated Soviet officer, I became isolated from my peers.

BBC News reported on November 4, 1956: "Soviet troops overrun Hungary. The Soviet air force has bombed part of the Hungarian capital, Budapest, and Russian troops have poured into the city in a massive dawn offensive. At least 1,000 Soviet tanks are reported to have entered Budapest."

Soviet tanks rolled into Budapest, killing thousands of young people, taking the city and, in but a few days, crushing the revolution. Refugees by the tens of thousands crossed the border to the West. One by one, the free Hungarian radio stations shut down, the last one heard in Munich: "If this message reaches the West, know that we will continue to fight for freedom." I felt devastated.

"The Soviets are right," chimed in one of my classmates, surprisingly of Hungarian extraction, "The strongest should prevail." With blinding fury, I knew I could "prevail" over him and knock him down, even though he towered over me. But by doing so, I would be no better than the Soviets who invaded Hungary. I held back.

The wave of demonstrations with lit candles that circled the world in support of the Hungarian Revolution soon gave way to gatherings in large New York venues, where speaker after speaker called for "peaceful coexistence" with the Soviet Union. And with its tanks, too? I wondered sarcastically. The media noted that at one such gathering, which I attended, there were a few "extremists" who agitated for freedom from the Soviet Union. Do you have to be an "extremist," I wondered, to long for freedom when foreign tanks overpower you? These meetings were searing to the soul. I was burning with anger at those who did not understand, who called for "peaceful coexistence" with the very power that had massacred thousands of young people.

There was the continuing burning sensation that the Free World could do so much if people only recognized what was going on in the countries behind the Iron Curtain. Conveying their devastating situation now became even more a matter of the utmost urgency, for we felt public opinion could influence the general attitude toward the Soviet Union and the measures the US government would take. The task was made all the more challenging because before the publication of Solzhenitsyn's *Gulag Archipelago* in 1973, much was written about those killed in Nazi camps but almost nothing was mentioned about the exterminations in the Soviet Union and its satellites. Those who survived were forbidden to speak of their experience, as I was to discover later.

A telling example was the document that Father Vasile Leu, who had been kidnapped in Vienna by the Soviet KGB (secret police) after his escape from Yugoslavia, was forced to sign after his release from the Aiud penitentiary in Romania:

> *La punerea mea în libertate din pentenţiarul Aiud, am luat cunoştinţă de faptul că nu am voe să divulg nimic din cele văzute şi auzite de mine in legătură cu locurile de deţinere pe unde am trecut şi nici despre deţinuţii rămaşi în locurile de deţinere.*

De asemeni nu voi comunica nimic scris sau verbal rudelor sau altor persoane despre deţinuţii rămaşi în locurile de deţinere.

In cazul că nu voi respecta cele arătate mai sus, am luat cunoştinţă de faptul că sunt pasibil a suporta rigorile legilor RPR.

Semnătură,
V. Leu

Data 1 august 1964 [32]

My translation:

Upon my liberation from the Aiud penitentiary [a maximum security penitentiary in Northwestern Romania], I was apprised of the fact that I was to disclose nothing of what I had seen or heard relating to the places where I had been detained nor about the detainees remaining in the places of detention.

Similarly, I will communicate nothing, in writing or orally, to relatives or other persons about the detainees remaining in the places of detention. Should I not respect the above, I was apprised of the fact that I am subject to the rigors of the RPR [Romanian People's Republic] laws.

Signed,
V. Leu

Date: August 1, 1964

An example, revealed 70 years later, shows how long the Soviets managed to keep secret their 1940 mass execution of about 22,000 Polish prisoners, mostly reserve officers, at Katyn in the Soviet Union:

[32]Paul Leu, *"Răpit de KGB şi condamnat la moarte"* (Euroland edition, Suceava 2009).

My peers and I were raised in a society so closely controlled by the Communists allied to the Soviet Union that the very mention of Katyn was prohibited. My wife spent her life wondering why her father, a doctor mobilized as a reserve officer in 1939, never came home.

It was only after the fall of Communism that she learned the truth, when President Boris Yeltsin of Russia gave Poles a list of prisoners to be executed at Katyn, including her father."

"Polish Heroes, Polish Victims"
—Wiktor Osiatynski
(*New York Times*, Op-Ed Friday, April 16, 2010)

Emilia Căzilă, an elderly Romanian of my parents' generation, refused to mention anything about her life in Romania, saying silence was the safest option. So did our friend Yolanda Kociumian's husband in New York. Upon hearing that I was writing what I remembered of my childhood experiences, Andrei Doneaud, the youngest student to be arrested when the Soviet troops arrived in Bucharest, said he could never do it for it would be too painful. Puiu Surducan, Father Surducan's son incarcerated with us at Kovačica and Zrenianin, has total amnesia about his time there. And I, even now, do not dare mention too much so as not to tire people or turn them away. Thus, the Communist regime stifled the passing of knowledge from one generation to the next in its effort to eliminate everything that could be antagonistic to it.

Sometimes I thought: All those who succeeded in reaching freedom in the United States, the Gulag survivors, the prisoners from Castro's Cuba and others, surely they will tell and write about it. But no. The horrible twist is that many were broken, or so pained that they could not speak or write about it—or so fearful still that they would not talk even in the safety of the United States.

Ignorance of the existence of this underworld of teeming suffering was bad enough. Even worse was its denial:

"Oh, the Communists cannot be that bad," had been repeatedly interjected in carefree lunchroom conversations at the French Lycée. "Give them a chance." "Don't believe her, they're prejudiced." "She should be ashamed to write such things" a Yugoslav schoolmate commented on my sister's recollection of our escape from Yugoslavia that was published in the school's yearbook. In geography classes, we were taught about the "miracle" of the Soviet economy, where Siberia's enormous natural wealth was being developed. But all along, the accounts of prisoners at Zrenianin returning from Siberia and the disaster they experienced there were ringing in my ears.

"Have the Communists harmed any of you?" asked my math teacher, a Communist sympathizer.

"Don't say anything, they might hurt you," my mother had warned. I cowered and kept quiet.

In time, haunted by my silence, I wondered whether my mother had been unduly scared. I don't believe there was any danger for me.

However, consider these cases, among many others:

- In 1977, our friend Monica Lovinescu, a writer in Paris much valued for conveying news from the Free World (forbidden in Romania) on Radio Free Europe, was beaten by Romanian Securitate thugs in her courtyard and left lying on the ground.
- In 1988, dissident Georgi Markov, a Communist defector from Bulgaria who worked for the BBC, was killed in London with ricin injected via an umbrella while he was waiting for a bus.[33]
- Also in 1988, Vlad Georgescu, working for Radio Free Europe in Germany, had been warned under threat of death not to broadcast excerpts from Ion Pacepa's book *Red Horizons*, a denunciation of Ceaușescu's regime. (The book had actually been photographed on the desk of President

[33]http://www.cnn.com/2003/WORLD/europe/01/07/terror.poison.bulgarian/.

George H. W. Bush.) Having ignored the threats, Vlad Georgescu was killed with a radioactive substance by the Securitate.[34]

- Even in 2006, such tactics were applied to Alexander Litvinenko, an officer with the Russian Federal Security Service (FSB) and a fierce critic of the Kremlin. He was killed in a London hotel with radioactive polonium 210.[35]

Yet if we do not say anything, who will?

As Dr. Jack Saul, psychologist at N.Y.U. Medical Center specializing in international trauma, noted, "Silence ultimately legitimizes violence and makes it more likely to occur in the future." He further pointed to "the difficulty to heal when our society, our officials, treat 'the torturers' as if they wielded legitimate political authority."[36]

But independent of any danger, speaking up was a challenge.

With an indulgent smile, obviously disbelieving my accounts of life under Soviet-imposed regimes, a friend asked, "What's the interest of a government to kill its own people? What is the interest of the Communists to ruin their own economy?"

What, indeed, is their interest?

Before the thundering collapse of the Soviet Union in 1991, at a time when the Soviet empire inspired respect in some, admiration in others, these questions made me feel powerless and reeling with frustration.

---

[34]See A. Ross Johnson and R. Eugene Parta, eds., *Impact on the Soviet Union and Eastern Europe* (Central European University Press, Budapest and New York, 2010, p. 218).

[35]"Inquiry Into Poisoning of Ex-K.G.B. Officer Opens in Britain, Alexander Litvinenko's Death Examined as Ties Fray Between Russia and West" by Alan Cowell (*BBC Magazine*, July 28, 2015).

[36]CNN, *World View*, January 26, 1998.

There Is No Corpse There

"There are no political prisoners whatsoever in the USSR" a distinguished Columbia University professor, freshly returned from a visit to the Soviet Union and its satellites, would assure us in 1960. He continued: "Nowhere does the government favor children's development as it does in Communist-controlled states."[37]

I thought of Kovačica and Zrenianin, where my little sister and I together with other children were incarcerated. And Romania, where in the 1950s 11-year old Florina Barbu and 11-year old Horia Blăgăilă had each, in different parts of the country, been beaten by the secret police in an effort to find out where their fathers were hiding. As an adult, Horia was haunted by the fact that he had not been able to resist and revealed his father's whereabouts. Also, 24,000 Greek children were forcefully torn away from their families by the Greek Communists and sent to the Soviet Union for "reeducation," some through the Bucharest train station where my mother and a Red Cross volunteer guided them on their way to their next destination.[38]

The distinguished professor never gave us a chance to ask any questions, even though he had promised a special session to do so.

"You are influenced by your personal experience" my friends would gently rebuff me when I gave examples contradicting the professor, as if personal experience were a reason to disqualify one from bearing witness.

---

[37]"Life in the Satellites" (*Columbia Daily Spectator*, Letters, December 9, 1960).

[38]About the children abducted by the Greek Communist rebels during the Greek Civil War from 1946 to 1949 and scattered behind the Iron Curtain; see Nicholas Gage's memoir, *Eleni* (Random House, New York, 1983). Also Niki Karavasilis, *The Abducted Greek Children of the Communists: "Paidomazoma"* (Rosedog Press, December 2006) and François Roche, "*28,000 enfants kidnappés*" (*Tribunal de l''Histoire*, no date available).

The Soviets continued to incarcerate political prisoners well into the 1980s, as exemplified by the world-renowned case of Gulag survivor and later Deputy Prime Minister of Israel, Natan Sharansky, author of the memoir *Fear No Evil* (Random House, 1988), who was detained in the Soviet Union in dire conditions from 1977 to 1986. I dreaded the news headlines about the Soviet Union (the "kingdom of lies," as Sharansky characterized it) and the excruciatingly painful articles that contorted the truth and deepened the Soviet hold on the world.

I spent my teenage years, my youth, hearing teachers and colleagues extol the marvels effected in the part of the world whose terror we had escaped.

A painful event that occurs in the open—a divorce, the loss of a limb, a death in the family—is much easier to bear when friends and acquaintances sympathize and support you. A similar event that is hidden, that no one suspects or, worse, that no one believes, that is denied, or that is treated not as a loss but, on the contrary, as a benefit is almost unbearable. Comments such as: "Look at the progress in your country thanks to the Soviet system, television, industrialization" ignore the fact that industrialization *did* exist in Romania before the Soviets occupied it and television *did* exist outside the Soviet world as well without the Soviets' help.

A priest, working with battered children in Denver, compared our predicament to that of his wards who attempt, in vain, to alert adults to their ordeal. He explained with the following image: as a frightened child points to a corpse lying on the ground, the disbelieving adults insist: **"No, there is no corpse there."** That was us.

Will the Truth Ever Come Out?

"A lie told often enough becomes the truth," Lenin is said to have stated. Can one hide the truth forever? Will the truth ever come out? Will it ever be acknowledged? At a time when no one could have suspected the collapse of the Soviet Union, this question tormented me incessantly.

Later I was to learn about the massive effort of disinformation to the West and the Soviet brainwashing.[39] But in the 1950s and 1960s, none of that had surfaced. The feeling that truth would forever be buried—that hell would never show its true face—crushed me as I grew up. "I know things other people don't know and I must live with that knowledge . . . I know things other people don't know and I must live with that knowledge . . . I know things other people don't know and I must live with that knowledge."

A vertiginous abyss gaped between our world "here" and our past life "there," drowning the possibility of communication between us and people in the West, even between us and earlier refugees, such as Mircea (my future husband), who had not experienced the full brunt of Communist oppression in Romania. Newer waves of refugees have the same complaint about us: "You left too long ago. You lost the gut feeling of the true situation there: the deceit, the humiliation, the lack of human integrity and dignity; the insidious psychological perversion of human nature when people are pressured into turning in to the regime their co-workers, neighbors, friends, even family; arbitrary laws that are impossible to obey; and the resultant constant atmosphere of guilt felt by people who are struggling to survive economically."

Influenced by my Western friends, I always hoped that things were not quite that dire in Romania. I wanted to believe it. I tried to believe it, I did my best to believe it, for it would have provided welcome relief. Invariably, though, attestations to the contrary from more recent refugees shattered my hope.

The crushing of the Hungarian Revolution in 1956, just as I was preparing to graduate from high school, put an end to all my hopes of liberation. The launch of the first artificial satellite, the Soviet Sputnik,

---

[39]See Edward Griffin's 1985 interview of Yuri Bezmenov.

in October 1957 rendered meaningless my dreams of space exploration—dreams nurtured avidly by reading the books of Pierre Rousseau (the French astronomer who popularized astronomy for children) while on the steamship *Ile de France* that took us to the new world when I was not yet twelve. There was no way I would be part of journeys beyond our planet if they were led by a monstrous power. What path to follow?

9

EXPANDING MY HORIZONS WITHIN THE PERSISTENT SOVIET GRIP

In May 1958, I graduated from the French Lycée in New York with honors, in my mind "for the sake of Romania." I was ready, but Romania was not. It was still occupied, still under the heel of the Communist dictatorship, unshaken by the Hungarian Revolution or by the demonstrations within the country itself. There was no end in sight. No end in sight.

My parents' generation, who had been so hopeful in France that the occupation could not last more than a few years, were now accepting the fact that the wait would have to be much, much longer. It slowly became apparent that Romania would not be freed in a matter of a few years, nor in my young adulthood. In time, my parents came to think they would not live to see the end of the Communist regimes in our land.

College and US Citizenship

I had to redirect my sights and my energy. I had to become a US citizen. Yale Professor Roberto Gonzalez Echevarria summed up my own feelings about my identity at that time in his *New York Times* op-ed piece many years later:

> *Though many Cubans in circumstances similar to mine became American citizens at the first opportunity, wisely aware that their displacement was permanent, I refused to do so because I naively associated citizenship and nationality. . . .Travel through Europe and Latin America required an assortment of visas, but I thought the difficulties were worth it because they allowed me to preserve my identity. (January 7, 2011)*

I, too, was prepared to face such difficulties, for I felt it an act of disloyalty to Romania to swear allegiance to the United States and to no other country, as was required for US citizenship in 1958. I loved the United States. I loved all it stood for—the opportunity to be free, to start life over again, to grow new roots. I loved the exhilarating feeling that anything was possible in the United States. I loved the American openness, kindness, and generosity I found here. But I felt intensely loyal to my origins—to the people, the language, the culture that had given me life and shape. So, like Professor Echevarria, I had contemplated not acquiring US citizenship. But, for a reason I still do not understand, this stance made me feel uneasy and almost ashamed. After my eighteenth birthday, I took the oath to become, in the words of the instruction booklet, "not a hyphenated American, not an Italian-American or a Polish-American or a Chinese-American, but an American."

Ahead now lay college and the tantalizing vistas it opened up. They filled me suddenly with optimism and exhilaration and proved wrong the conviction I had absorbed from the French culture, mistakenly or not, that happiness does not really exist. I was living it!

Floating with hope and curious to discover the challenge of an American education and the experiences that were apt to unfold, I dove with enthusiasm and anticipation into this new world. Because of my accomplishments at the French Lycée, and at my father's insistence, I was accepted at New York's Barnard College as a junior.

THE UNITED STATES OF AMERICA

ORIGINAL
TO BE GIVEN TO
THE PERSON NATURALIZED

CERTIFICATE OF NATURALIZATION

No. 8013663

Petition No. 697232

Personal description of holder as of date of naturalization: Date of birth May 31, 1940 sex female complexion medium color of eyes brown color of hair brown height 5 feet 2 inches; weight 105 pounds; visible distinctive marks none
Marital status single former nationality Roumanian
I certify that the description above given is true, and that the photograph affixed hereto is a likeness of me.

Ingrid Alina Popa
(Complete and true signature of holder)

UNITED STATES OF AMERICA
SOUTHERN DISTRICT OF NEW YORK ss:

Be it known, that at a term of the District Court of The United States held pursuant to law at New York City on April 7, 1958 the Court having found that Ingrid Alina Popa then residing at 1025 Fifth Avenue, New York, N.Y. intends to reside permanently in the United States (when so required by the Naturalization Laws of the United States), had in all other respects complied with the applicable provisions of such naturalization laws, and was entitled to be admitted to citizenship, thereupon ordered that such person be and (s)he was admitted as a citizen of the United States of America.

In testimony whereof the seal of the court is hereunto affixed this 7th day of April in the year of our Lord nineteen hundred and 58 and of our Independence the one hundred and 82nd

Seal

It is a violation of the U.S. Code (and punishable as such) to copy, print, photograph, or otherwise illegally use this certificate.

HERBERT A. CHARLSON
Clerk of the U.S. District Court
By [illegible] Deputy Clerk.

DEPARTMENT OF JUSTICE

My certificate of naturalization, April 7, 1958.

If there is one thing I regret in my life, it is having cut short my college experience. This involved having to declare a major immediately, without a chance to transition from French to English, to adjust to the culture of the United States, to explore the plethora of possibilities that spread out in front of me, and to make informed choices.

Guided by my French teachers, for whom mathematics was the basis of all studies, I opted for mathematics after briefly considering a career in medicine. I discarded that option, though, having already witnessed too much suffering and not wanting to be exposed to more as a doctor. Casting only a fleeting glance at electronic music in Prof. Otto Luening's classes, at Petrarch's poetry unfolded by Prof. Maristella Lorch, at Oliver Wendell Holmes's *Autocrat of the Breakfast Table* in English Literature class, and at some basic economics and biology notions, I immersed myself in mathematics, without having a chance to explore the worlds that a college education would be laying in front of me.

While I was steeped in my studies, Fidel Castro came to campus. The student body gave him a rousing reception. At the same time a few Cuban refugees present in the crowd proffered accounts of the situation in Communist Cuba that eerily paralleled that in Romania, even though an ocean and a continent separated the two countries. Everyone else around me brushed aside the refugees' accounts.

"No, there is no corpse there."

Within days of my twentieth birthday, in June 1960, I graduated with a B.A. in mathematics from Barnard College.

What next???

Adrift, and Then a Triple Crown

With all my soul, I had waited for Romania to be free again and to help rebuild it; that aspiration had kept us all going. Now I realized that nothing was changing in the Soviet world and feared that for the rest of my life I would have to strive to accept the fact that never again would I see the land whence I came. I had felt I could give up my life for the liberation of Romania were that exchange possible, but now my momentum was cut short. Like a ship forging ahead at full steam when the power is suddenly cut off, I was left adrift with no direction in sight.

That's when I lost my life compass. I realized I was no longer part of the world that surrounded me. I felt disoriented, cut off from planet Earth by a glass sphere through which I watched, below, humanity go about its business.

To give up helping Romania without a meaningful activity to replace it was to accept a huge void within myself.

No amount of studying, certainly not mathematics, could fill that void nor counter the emotional charge stemming from the reality of the present world. The devastation and continuing mass killings (20 million in the Soviet Union alone and 65 million in China)[40] left me bereft for I was powerless to do anything about it and people around me were blissfully unaware of it. Life stopped having a meaning and I fell prey to insomnia, to nightmares of floating in underground streams in narrow caves about to be engulfed by the earth. I led a dead life.

Yet I had to go on living. I had to find another meaning for my life.

After a year of exploring various possibilities, none of which—not the study of astronomy at Columbia University, nor a job offer at IBM—presented me with a meaningful application of my training, I decided to persevere in mathematics in the form of a master's degree in pure mathematics, Columbia University's forte and my (useless) love. Eventually, I gave in to the lure of a climb to the top of the mountain—a doctorate, savoring its challenge every step along the way.

Within a few years (1969–1972), I reached a triple crown: the joy and deep satisfaction of marriage to Mircea Fotino, a US citizen of Romanian origin and French culture, just like me; the exhilaration of a PhD in mathematics from New York University's Courant Institute of Mathematical Sciences (even though my concentration in algebra and number theory still had no real-world applications); and the immeasurable blessing of the birth of our first child, a daughter named Domnica, two months after we left the East Coast to settle in Colorado.

In the meantime, the Soviet Union tightened its grip on the lands it occupied and Soviet propaganda deepened its tentacles, especially in the media and in academia. As an example, a fellow student at the Courant Institute had been moved by the "generosity of the Soviets"

---

[40]See *The Black Book of Communism,: Crimes, Terror, Repression* by Jean-Louis Panné, Andrzej Paczkowski, Karel Bartosek, et al. (Harvard University Press, Cambridge, MA, 1999, p. 4). This book documents the following conservative estimates of the Communist genocide: USS.R.: 20 million deaths; China: 65 million deaths; Vietnam: 1 million deaths; North Korea: 2 million deaths; Cambodia: 2 million deaths (a quarter of its population); Eastern Europe: 1 million deaths; Latin America: 150,000 deaths; Africa: 1.7 million deaths; and Afghanistan: 1.5 million deaths.

who launched a rocket in 1969 concomitantly with Apollo XI because, in her opinion, "They did it to help the American astronauts should they encounter difficulties on their way to the moon"! (After the collapse of the Soviet Union, it came to light that the Soviets had fiercely strived to beat the United States in their "race to the moon," even launching a last-ditch rocket in parallel with that of the United States.)

It became increasingly apparent that, contrary to the Nazi empire that had dissolved, the Soviet Union was here to stay—an integral and sanctioned part of the family of nations.

Integrating

I had to drastically change course, to merge my old drive into the new ways and perspectives of the land in which I now lived, to transition to life on this continent.

I had to integrate. But how? By giving up my ways and my identity to assume a new persona? By distancing myself from exiled Romanians and from my parents to dive into unfamiliar grounds? Some refugees, following this line of thought, forgot the Romanian language, changed their names and their religion, and became thoroughly American. To do the same, I would have to give up my mother tongue—the one thing after the Soviets took our homes, our families, and our country, after they distorted our culture and our past—the one thing left to keep them from eliminating us altogether,[41] the one thing I was absolutely resolved not to surrender.

Other refugees entered the job market, earned a good living in the United States while maintaining their language and their customs and

[41] For example, in the Romanian province of Bessarabia (present-day Republic of Moldova), the language spoken by the local (Romanian) population was declared by the Soviets to be "Moldovan." To this day, some Western media refer to Moldovan as an independent language, even though no "Moldovan–Romanian" dictionary exists since they are one and the same language. It would be like referring to the language spoken in Colorado as "Coloradan."

never became fluent in English, never assimilated in the local population—they forever would remain outsiders in the land in which they lived out the rest of their days. For me, this would have meant being forever a foreigner in the country that accepted us, that gave us a new lease on life, and toward which my gratitude is immense.

But there were also those—and I eventually married one of them—who grew roots here while also remaining faithful to themselves and to their traditions, who were enlarging their horizons with several new languages and cultures, assimilating them all with gusto, at ease and fluent in them all. That became my solution of predilection.

Still, it presented enormous obstacles: How to integrate among people whose experience is as foreign to mine as mine is to theirs and whose feelings and thinking are a mystery to me?

Cambodian refugee Sathaya Tor, who had experienced the Cambodian genocide of a quarter of the population between 1975 and 1978,[42] said succinctly: "Sometimes I feel kind of isolated emotionally. We're just from different worlds, and it's hard to mix them together."[43] These words reflected my own feeling of being adrift in my new home.

How can anyone who just experienced a traumatic loss of homeland, especially if the conditions that devastated it continue, get excited about a baseball game, a rock concert, a new fad, or even about local politics? All would seem revoltingly trivial in view of a homeland situation that continued to be harrowing, jabbing at one's soul and keeping the wound open.

Corporal Steven Crawford, a returning Iraq prisoner, had commented: "I always hear people complain about stuff, and it just makes me mad because a lotta people don't understand. They don't see the

---

[42] *The Black Book of Communism* (Harvard University Press, Cambridge, MA, 1999).
[43] "From Cambodia Captive to Prep School Scholar" (*New York Times*, June 8, 1987).

stuff that—they just go about their daily lives, while there's still people dyin' every day. For them. And it— it upsets me a lot."[44]

Should such a person speak about his or her world, "normal" people would not understand and eventually tire of it. So the person "integrates," discusses baseball and fads and local politics, but only superficially, floating above the heavy, stifling, crushing, burning weight that is still there, year in and year out until it is addressed.

Or, as eventually happened to me decades later in Colorado, until it was shared with compassionate friends who took the time to listen with their hearts. Or until first-born Domnica started laboriously to write "your" story, which she heard from us. Or until Adriana (born five years after Domnica, with the same difference in age as that between my sister and me) initiated me to the wonders of her American education, allowing me to graft her experience as an eight-year-old onto mine and relive that part of my childhood in the rich, vibrant, fulfilling setting of the Flatirons School in Boulder, Colorado.

Until that happened, however, I was faced with having to integrate in the present, even among people I did not understand and who did not understand me. But how?

Reality Versus the US Perception of the Soviet Union

Rather than striving to be understood, I concentrated on understanding the people in this country myself.

Having been raised in French schools, I was unaware of the political charge the word "Communist" carried in the 1950s and 1960s in the United States, where the terrain was seeded with local turmoil and passions. Strong reactions were provoked by McCarthyism, named for its protagonist US Senator Joseph McCarthy, who essentially adopted

---

[44]From the interview "Operation Proper Exit: A Return to the War Zone" on *60 Minutes* (CBS, November 6, 2011).

Communist methods to fight Communism (therefore defeating his purpose). Similarly, liberals reacted strongly to the anti-Communism of conservatives, turning them into anti-anti-Communists, with everyone totally unaware of the reality of Communism behind the Iron Curtain.

I also understood that, simultaneously, Communism was viewed by some in the United States as an extension of liberalism and socialism, and hence desirable. As Zbigniew Brzezinski, National Security Advisor to US President Jimmy Carter, explained shortly before the entire Soviet edifice was to crumble, "to the extent that the new Bolshevik rulers were able to identify themselves with socialism, it helped enormously in gaining a sympathetic hearing in the West,"[45] when in fact the Soviet camp represented a merciless oppression that systematically disregarded human values or morality.

Add to that people who desired to hang onto their hopes and ideals and found it difficult to accept an unpleasant reality. *The God that Failed*,[46] in which six authors recount their dreams of Communism and their rude awakening, made me grasp the thirst, the need to believe in a better, more just world. Some associated such a world with their ideal concept of Communism while keeping a safe distance from its reality. Those in my surroundings who desired to promote economic well-being and social justice for all created a pervasive atmosphere of sympathy for Communism, in which even I felt sometimes ashamed about my gut reaction against it.

Finally, one more obstacle to grasping the Soviet reality is the fact that, during World War II, the Soviet Union was an ally of the United States—a necessity, perhaps, imposed by the Nazi aggression. Contrary

---

[45]Zbigniew Brzezinski, *The Grand Failure: The Birth and Death of Communism in the Twentieth Century* (Charles Scribner's Sons, New York, 1989, p. 18).

[46]Arthur Koestler, Ignazio Silone, Richard Wright, André Gide, Louis Fischer, and Stephen Spender, *The God that Failed* (Richard Crossman, Ed., Columbia University Press, New York, 2001).

to the Nazi regime, the Soviet Union was not defeated in war and its documents were not released to the world. Its officials could continue to keep them secret, doctoring them or destroying them as they deemed advantageous to their cause. Much worse, officials in the United States seemed reluctant—almost fearful—to anger the leaders of the Soviet Union, as illustrated by the notorious massacre of about 22,000 Polish officers in 1940 in the Katyn forest of Western Russia.

Katyn Massacre Cover-up in Both the USSR and the US

The Soviets attributed the Katyn massacre to Germany, even though those of us from Central and Eastern Europe knew the Polish prisoners were executed by the Soviets. Only decades later, in 1990, under President Boris Yeltsin and on the eve of the fall of the Soviet Union, did the Soviets acknowledge that they were the perpetrators of the massacre. The European Court of Human Rights and the 1951 Madden Committee of the US House of Representatives confirmed these facts:

- The European Court of Human Rights says Russia has failed to explain why it kept key files secret when it investigated the 1940 Katyn massacre of more than 20,000 Polish war prisoners.
- Russia failed to comply with a human rights obligation to provide evidence, the Strasbourg judges ruled. (BBC News/World–Europe, 21 October 2013).

Simultaneously, the US government under President Franklin D. Roosevelt tried to cover up the deed:

- New evidence appears to back the idea that the Roosevelt administration helped cover up Soviet guilt for the 1940 Katyn massacre of Polish soldiers. Historians said documents, released by the US National Archives, supported the suspicion that the US did not want to anger its wartime ally, Joseph Stalin. (BBC News/World–Europe, 11 September 2012; http://www.bbc.com/ news/world-europe-19552745).

From a Department of State document, declassified in 2011:[47]

- The [1951] Madden Committee determined unanimously that the NKVD [USSR secret police, predecessor of the KGB] was responsible for the [Katyn] executions and recommended a trial before the International World Court of Justice. The question of an American cover-up was less clear cut. In its final report, the committee concluded that American officials failed to properly evaluate and act upon clear danger signals in Russian behavior evident as early as 1942. In addition, the committee found that *American policy toward the Soviet Union might have been different if information deliberately withheld from the public had been made available sooner.* [my emphasis]

Czech dissident Václav Havel and his colleagues emphasized: "If the main pillar of the system is living a lie, then it is not surprising that the fundamental threat to it is living the truth. This is why it [the truth] must be suppressed more severely than anything else." (*The Power of the Powerless, Citizens Against the State in Central-Eastern Europe*, Václav Havel et al., M.E. Sharpe, Armonk, NY, 1985, p. 40).

Eventually, evidence of KGB fabrications, referred to as "disinformation," appeared in the media,[48] as well as evidence of

---

[47]Record Group 59, General Records of the Department of State, Central Decimal File, 1940-1944, box 2919, folder 740.00116 EW/1010 53 [National Archives Identifier 302021], http://www.archives.gov/research/foreign-policy/katyn-massacre/index.html.

[48]FBI: Evidence likely faked by David Rising and Randy Herschaft of the Associated Press in the *Denver Post*, April 13, 2011. Also "Soviet news fabrications attack US" by (Associated Press, *Denver Post*, August 18, 1987.

false documents meant to smear those who had anti-Communist stances.[49]

The Truth Comes Out

Gradually, the general attitude toward the Soviet Union started to change in the United States and around the world, easing somewhat the load I had carried for so many years.

It took the filming of Boris Pasternak's *Dr. Zhivago* in 1965, as well as the publication of Alexandr Solzhenitsyn's *The First Circle* in 1968 and his Nobel Prize for Literature in 1970 to at last start shedding some light on the realities of the Soviet world that we survivors had been striving so eagerly and so unsuccessfully to convey over the years.

In the early 1960s, Alexander Solzhenitsyn's name had started hitting the newsstands with the 1962 publication of *One Day in the Life of Ivan Denisovich*, about life in a Soviet prison camp. He had dared write about the hidden, buried truths of life in the Soviet Union and thus created a stir. Similar wavelets had surfaced earlier when Yugoslav dissident Milovan Djilas revealed the existence of a privileged ruling "new class" in 1957 that took hold in Communist regimes.[50] Solzhenitsyn's stature, however, reached much greater heights.

With the publication of his *The First Circle*, which delved into life under Stalin, the wave was becoming a tide. Wielding the authority of a man still captive in the Soviet Union, revealing the genius of a first-rate author, Solzhenitsyn's voice became ever louder and swept the

---

[49]For example, the campaign to smear Prix Goncourt Laureate Vintila Horia, whose award-winning book, *God Was Born in Exile* (St. Marten's Press, Paris, 1960; English translation 1961) is a portrayal of dictatorships.

[50]This privilege was to be humorously illustrated during Nicolae Ceauşescu's 1970 official visit to the White House. In deference to the Socialist sensitivities of the Communist leader, guests were asked to wear modest attire; in particular, ladies were to forgo long dresses. One can imagine their surprise and disappointment when Elena Ceauşescu appeared in a stunning floor-length gown looking straight out of the best Parisian fashion houses.

world into an awareness of all I wanted to say but did not know how. He was the man I had unknowingly been praying for. Solzhenitsyn had the facts, the age, the maturity, the fabulous memory, the talent, the will, the drive to "say it as it is," and he did just that. He relieved from my shoulders the burden of "letting the world know" at a time when I felt like a preacher without a tongue. He pierced the festering wound in my heart, relieved it of the deeply ingrained, despairing frustration accumulated over the years and started slowly to alleviate the crushing weight that had pressed on my chest all these years.

Simultaneously, dramatic upheavals started shaking and waking up the world.

- 1968: *Soviet tanks rolled into Czechoslovakia* in reaction to the liberalization of the Communist regime in the country, the so-called "Prague Spring." The population watched in silence as their peaceful revolution was overwhelmed.
- 1975: *Cambodian genocide was committed by the Communist Khmer Rouge*, led by French-educated Pol Pot, with chilling images on television of the stream of human beings being led out of the cities, some dragged out of hospitals, into the fields. Their aim was to create a "ground zero" on which to build a new society.[51] The most widely accepted estimate of the number of people who were killed or died as a result of this forced exodus is about one-quarter of the Cambodian population. As reported in the *Denver Post*, April 16, 1998: "Up to 2 million Cambodians [out of a population of 7 million] died through mass executions, disease and starvation during the mid-seventies."

[51]"On April 17, 1975, . . . Khmer Rouge soldiers captured Phnom Pen and Battambang and began a massive evacuation of every city and town. The men, women, and children who weren't slaughtered immediately were herded into labor camps where they faced torture, disease, starvation, exhaustion and death." (*Rocky Mountain News*, June 25, 2004).

These horrors elicited the following casual comment from one of my closest, generous, liberal friends: “Oh that’s the Cambodian way, every few centuries they have a blood bath.”

Dith Pran, the Cambodian journalist who experienced first-hand the killing fields,[52] says he needs to keep on speaking: “I feel each man has his destiny. If God permitted this, it is for me to share my experience. If I survived, I must bear witness.”

So must I.

Even after the world outcry following the Hungarian and Czecho-slovak revolutions in 1956 and 1958, respectively, after the shock of the Cambodian genocide in 1975, the official recognition by Western governments of those who perpetrated these deeds continued.

The grip of the Soviet Union seemed solidly entrenched in the world and manifested itself again, this time in Afghanistan.

- 1979: *Soviet invasion of Afghanistan.*
- 1984: *Afghan children deported to the Soviet Union.* The year 1984 heralded a series of kidnappings reminiscent of the more than 20,000 Greek children abducted in the 1940s by the Greek Communists and deported to various countries behind the Iron Curtain.[53]

The heart-rending images of children being torn from their mothers’ arms to be deported to the Soviet Union for indoctrination was reported in the *New York Times* “Around the World,” on November 14, 1984:

> *Western diplomats said today that the Soviet authorities in Afghanistan had begun a program to send thousands of*

[52] *The Killing Fields* (1984) is a motion picture based on his experience.

[53] François Broche reports the following “*Les rapports de la Croix Rouge avaint fourni une estmation relativement précise: en tout 26 500 enfants avaiet été enlevés. Six pays... se les partgeaient: la Yougoslavie (11 000), la Roumanire (6 500), la Tchécoslovaquie (3 500), la Hongrie (3 000), la Bulgarie (2 000) et la Pologne (500).*” (“Tribunal de l’ Histoire,” p. 116.)

primary-school Afghan children to the Soviet Union for at least 10 years of indoctrination into Communism and the Soviet way of life. The diplomats said 870 Afghan children, aged 7 to 9, left for Soviet Central Asia in the first such flight on Nov. 5.

From yet another account, "Afghanistan: The Sorrow of Parting," in *Time* magazine on November 26, 1984:

The scene at Kabul airport was heartrending, according to one observer: parents and relatives were held at gunpoint behind police barricades, prevented from gathering their departing children in a final embrace. Amid tears and anguish, earlier this month some 370 Afghan children between the ages of seven and nine were herded aboard a Soviet airliner. Their destination: the Soviet Union, where for the next 15 to 20 years they will be put through a course of political indoctrination. According to the official voice of Afghan President Babrak Karmal's Soviet-backed regime, the children will be taught "Marxist–Leninist thinking, and an appreciation of the greatness of the Soviet state and the evils of imperialism."

Although hard statistics are difficult to find, M. Siddieq Noorzoy, Emeritus Professor of Economics at the University of Alberta, offers this estimate: "Soviet forces kidnapped an estimated 50,000 Afghan children from villages, orphanages, and city streets in an effort to indoctrinate them in Communist ideology and use them to form militias."

Preparing my little daughters for bed at night and glimpsing their delicate, vulnerable torsos, I was horrified by the thought of what it means to have one's children torn away.

Some of our acquaintances' reactions, not too uncommon at the time, included, "Afghanistan is in the Soviets' backyard. They must defend themselves." From what?

This time, though, there was some reaction from the President of the United States: Jimmy Carter canceled the US participation at the 1980 Olympic games to be held in Moscow.

As people's perceptions of the Soviet Union started changing, they became more receptive to our experience and to accounts of the continued distress behind the Iron Curtain. The burden of isolation was becoming lighter.

Liberation of Political Prisoners in Romania under US Pressure

Starting in the early 1960s, under pressure from the United States, the situation in Romania had undergone several changes; one was particularly dramatic: To obtain "most favored nation" status (which would give Romania trade advantages with the United States), Gheorghe Gheorgiu-Dej, the head of Romania, agreed to release Romania's political prisoners. Prisons were practically emptied of thousands of prisoners. My Uncle Horia finally came home after 16 years of incarceration, during the last of which he had absolutely no contact with his family. They did not even know whether he was still alive.

Under Ceaușescu, the Iron Curtain became slightly less rigid. In an understanding with Germany, Romanian citizens who had a German family connection were allowed to emigrate to Germany. Thus, in 1981, my cousin Adrian, whose mother-in-law was German, settled in Bonn. And in 1985 my cousin Mihai and my childhood friend Anca succeeded in escaping and settling in France. This was our first chance to meet family members and to capture echoes from beyond the Iron Curtain. Traveling to Europe to meet them was one of the high points of my life.

10

ECHOES FROM BEYOND THE IRON CURTAIN: 1,000 COUSINS

In the summer of 1985, Mircea and I took off, along with our daughters, to meet two of my seven first cousins as well as my dearest childhood friend, Anca. I had neither seen nor spoken with them since 1948, thirty-seven years earlier. In Paris, we met Mihai (the son of my father's brother Valter) and Anca. In Bonn, we met Adrian (the son of my father's sister Helga). It turned out to be a momentous reunion.

"*Let me see my cousin!*" Mihai's booming voice preceded him into the room, then we flew into each other's arms.

My eyes welled up at this unexpected greeting, because my cousins were part of an extended family in Romania who did not need me nor even know me, but I needed them for they were my roots.

Mihai, the former 3-year-old I remembered with a shock of luminous blond curls, was now dark-haired and close in size to my petite frame. Down-to-earth, with a glimmer of humor in his face reminiscent of his father, Mihai teased me about my emotion. He then warmed my heart by offering to drive the five hours that separated Paris from Bonn to meet Adrian, whom I had glimpsed before our escape as an infant lying on my parents' bed in Romania.

Talking all the way to Bonn, Mihai explained that my father's existence had saved him from the pressure of joining the Communist Party, as his uncle's presence in the West would have been a stain on his record as a Party member.

For his escape in 1982 across the Danube that formed the border between Romania and Yugoslavia, Mihai had picked August 23, a national holiday observed by the Communist regime,[54] during which the guards were doubled, meaning they would patrol in pairs and so would be less attentive. Having trained for years in endurance swimming, Mihai crossed the mountains bordering the Danube on foot to the spot he had chosen for his escape, near the Herculean Baths (the site of our escape so many decades earlier), by scrutinizing a 15-meter-long map of the Danube provided by our grandfather. As night fell, he entered the water and started swimming. About halfway to the other shore, a patrol boat appeared. He ducked its headlights under water. About four hours after starting his swim, he reached the Yugoslav shore, simultaneously with two other swimmers (over two thousand people were said to have escaped so far across the Danube that year). There was a brief exchange of fire between the Yugoslav border patrol and the Romanian patrol on the boat. One of the other refugees was wounded. In the darkness of night, Mihai was caught by the Yugoslav guards.

It turned out that Adrian had been part of Mihai's planned escape. He was to wait for Mihai at the spot where he expected to end his swim. He drove on shabby roads to the Yugoslav shore of the Danube, settled in a parking lot with his headlights on to dispel suspicion and waited. But Mihai was captured. Through the connections of his German

[54]August 23, 1944, is the day when young King Michael, with the support of representatives of the main political parties (the National Peasant Party, the National Liberal Party, the Social Democratic Party), as well as of the Romanian Communist Party, led a coup against strongman Ion Antonescu and switched sides, joining the Allies against Germany. The Communists considered it to be their victory.

mother-in-law, Adrian obtained the necessary papers to get Mihai released. Three weeks later Mihai arrived in Germany, and later he moved to France.

We discussed the difficulty of adapting to a new country and the various degrees to which different cousins gave up (or didn't give up) their heritage. Some cousins, for example, did not teach their children Romanian to spare them a foreign accent in their adoptive country. Mihai was convinced he could become totally French without in any way giving up our Romanian language or traditions. We were in sync.

We arrived at Adrian's in Bonn at 6 p.m.

Adrian opened the door. Dark-gold hair, dark-blue eyes, deep tan, brilliant smile, smashingly handsome, radiating warmth from his open arms, he embodied features of both his parents and more. I winced, hard put to sustain the emotion of this additional encounter.

Adrian's family surrounded him: his wife Anda, the daughter of Vlad Călinescu, one of Mircea's closest friends, now deceased; her mother Ilse; and two adorable blond sons, Mati, 6 years old, and Alex, 4.

Even though most of us had never met before, it soon became obvious we felt like a tight-knit family, unchanged by the decades-long separation and lack of communication. But just like Mihai, Adrian's family could not quite grasp my emotion at seeing them. We talked until 2:30 in the morning. Domnica and Adriana, sustained by an intense curiosity, lasted until 11 p.m.

Before approaching the more painful questions, my cousins, bantering and joking, admitted that, in our serious, studious, duty-driven family, they fit more in the black sheep category. In his youth, Mihai played the guitar in a band instead of joining a classical group like the senior Popa brothers' string and piano trio (with my father at the piano). Adrian, raised by a work-exhausted mother without the guidance of his incarcerated father, would slip out of the apartment at

From left to right: Adrian's wife Anda; my cousin Mihai, me, my cousin Adrian, Mircea.

night and return when all had left for the day. When his father was finally released from prison, he attempted to discipline his rebellious 16-year-old son, but to no avail. Now aged 37, Adrian had the greatest pride and appreciation for his father.

Sharing family recollections, I was delighted to discover that O'Papa, our grandfather, who proved pivotal in my childhood, inspired in my cousins the same very deep attachment I felt. They surprised me when they mentioned that, while I was longing for them, they were striving to imagine their cousins in America.[55]

Adrian was perplexed by his brother Emanuel's refusal to emigrate, like him, to Germany. Emanuel, however, felt it was important to maintain our culture and traditions within Romania.

---

[55]Later I was to learn that, at tea parties organized for my numerous cousins by my Aunt Clementina Holban (my father's first cousin) together with her mother, Eugenia Lescovar, a photograph of my sister and me was always present.

They mentioned Lydia, my mother's sister, who took Helga with little Emanuel and Adrian into her apartment in 1950 when the Communist government expelled them from their own apartment while their father was still in prison and threw their belongings into the street. No one other than Lydia had dared come to their assistance, as the risk of having contact with the families of political prisoners was too great.

Soon thereafter, Lydia's turn came to be arrested for having harbored an Eastern Catholic priest in her apartment.[56] Released after a few months, she was incarcerated a second time, in 1951, for close to four years, at the Mislea prison for women. Upon her final release in 1955, she had no idea whether Helga was still in her apartment and whether she would have a place to stay. To her immense relief, Helga was still there. The first night, the boys slept on chairs to make room for her. They found her very tense, restless, and fearful.

I dove earnestly into the subject of Uncle Horia's imprisonment, trying thus to understand my own. Adrian, like Mihai earlier, jested about my eagerness. They obviously could have no sense of how deeply prison had affected me. Mihai had himself asked Uncle Horia about torture and he responded: "When I'll tell you, for example, that we were made to eat a bowl of feces by the spoonful, you'll realize you don't want to hear about torture." Still Adrian willingly assented. What he told me about his father's experience was beyond what I could imagine.

For example, conditions were so dire that, close to the ground, nets were extended along the prison walls to catch those who attempted suicide. At one point, Uncle Horia was locked in a dark, cold, moist cell that prisoners didn't usually survive. "We don't want to kill you," he was assured. "What we want is to destroy your psyche." This is the

[56]Father Vesa, possibly also Father Leluțiu. Catholic and Eastern Catholic (or Uniate) priests were persecuted at that time, and some went into hiding.

principle behind what is called "reeducation." Reeducated prisoners were then sent into society to convince people to cooperate with the government.

Our grandfather's intervention on Uncle Horia's behalf with Romania's Communist head of state, Gheorghe Gheorghiu-Dej, was to no avail, even though he had reminded the leader that he had put his daughters through school while he was himself imprisoned in the early 1930s as a Communist protest instigator. "The Soviets oppose it" our grandfather was told. Only the pressure of the US President Lyndon Johnson, negotiating the possibility of granting Romania most-favored-nation status, resulted in the release, in 1964, of thousands of political prisoners, including Uncle Horia.

Uncle Horia had survived, unbroken, for 16 years. When he came home, instead of staring at a TV set or at a wall, as many others did after a few years of incarceration, he started painting and counseling priests, his sense of humor intact. What gave him such strength? Is religion a sufficient explanation? This question had haunted me for years until I finally found the answer when we went to Romania after the collapse of the Communist regime.

The next morning Adrian moved me deeply by handing me authenticated copies of our grandparents' birth certificates. For decades I had no tangible proof whatsoever of their existence or of that of anyone in our family. I absorbed much strength and balance from this encounter. It was as if the legs that supported me had been cut off and now at least one leg was propped under me.

At 11:00 a.m., we left for our return trip to Paris.

Seven-year-old Adriana wrote in our travel diary: "Yesterday we went to Bonn to see my cousins and my mom's cousin. It was the first time I've ever seen any cousins."

"1,000 cousins!" exclaimed thirteen-year-old Domnica.

So Many Years to Catch Up On

Even more emotional was my reunion with Anca.

Amazingly, the same year Mihai escaped across the Danube, Anca escaped to Greece by an incredible fluke, when her husband, Boris Stuparu, attended an architects' conference in Athens. The fluke took the shape of a mistake in that, contrary to the well-established government policy of not allowing professionals to attend meetings in foreign countries unless a member of their immediate family remained behind (a "hostage"), Anca and their twelve-year-old son were both granted a passport to accompany Boris to Greece. She could not believe it!

In Athens, they stayed with a former abducted Greek child[57] whom Boris had met at the university in Bucharest, and who, as an adult, chose to return to Greece. Their friend helped them obtain a permit to travel to France where they received political asylum, which allowed them to remain in the West.

Anca was now residing in Paris.

I was not sure I could face her. Anca and Tudor, the core of my childhood, the friends I had waited for months to see enter through the gate at Zrenianin, the friends I had dreamt of for years in Paris and in New York—I did not know how to face this encounter after all this time.

I rang the doorbell of her apartment at the Porte d'Italie, filled with both joy and apprehension. As the door opened, I could not look at Anca. I had so striven to imagine this moment. It was like looking at the sun. My gaze slipped away toward Adriana who stood next to me. Eventually, somehow, my eyes turned toward my friend.

Open, direct, affectionate, unimposing, Anca was better than all I remembered.

So many years to catch up on . . .

---

[57]One of the 24,000 children abducted by the Communist rebels during the Greek Civil War, from 1946 to 1949 and scattered behind the Iron Curtain.

To my surprise, Anca shared that, even while growing up in her familiar environment, she had nurtured the dream of leaving Romania. While we felt isolated in the West from everything we left behind, they felt exiled in their own country—culturally isolated in Romania from the "outside world," obliged to steep in the Soviet culture, cut off from French, Italian and all the forbidden Western influences with which we resonate.

Worse than the isolation was the weight of the lies she had to endure in the Communist system, the distortion of facts, the falsification of history. Like Mihai, she said she left because of these lies, because of the lack of quality of the people who ruled their lives, professional as well as personal. They depended on the least educated and the most morally low part of society.

Determined to find a way to leave, Anca bought no important piece of furniture, pasted no meaningful photographs in her albums, made no long-term plans. When she considered marriage to Boris, she warned him of her resolve. She worked on an escape for more than 20 years, almost succeeding several times. After their defection to Greece, there were consequences: for many months her mother was awakened around 2 o'clock in the morning by telephone calls with insults and threats, a constant torment. As for Tudor, he could no longer advance in his career.

The parallelism between our lives tightened our bond even more. We both felt isolated in our worlds and we both were weighed down by lies—I by the lies spread by the Soviets that I failed to counter in the West, and she by the lies inherent in the Soviet-imposed regime in Romania.

Back in the States: Exhilaration and Resignation

Back in the States in an emotional upheaval, I felt exultant. The refrain twirled nonstop in my brain: I found Anca. I found my cousins. I found Anca. I found my cousins. I found Anca. I found my cousins.

Furthering my contact with family, my second cousin Daniela, now a civil engineer in Chicago, arrived as a political refugee in the United States in 1985 as well. It had taken her four years of repeated requests and interviews with the Securitate to finally obtain permission to leave the country. The permission came at a price: she had to pledge to renounce everything she had in Romania, renounce any claim on property or on a job, and she was required to renounce her Romanian citizenship as well, for which coerced renunciation she had to pay the equivalent of a month's salary.

When I asked her if she regretted having left Romania, given her present hardship in raising her daughter alone after her divorce and her mother's death, her answer was an emphatic: "No! Never!!"

"Why not?"

"Because we all lived in fear, we could not go out of the country, there was *no hope*. The Communist system was so capricious that people never knew what further hardship might await them tomorrow." For example, in the heart of the bitterest winter in Bucharest, gas was turned off so there was no heat in their homes. Electricity was cut off several hours each day so they could not use electric heaters. They went to their attic in search for anything that could be burned in their stove, papers, old furniture, etc.

Other immigrants mentioned living and sleeping with coats, hats, and gloves on and cooking only at night during the few hours when gas was available, perhaps as a result of Ceaușescu's 1971 visit to North Korea. Also, he razed entire historic neighborhoods and their jewel-like churches to make room for his monumental "House of the People," said to be the second largest building in the world after the Pentagon, and its appurtenant constructions on the "Avenue of the Victory of Socialism." Meanwhile, grocery stores emptied steadily, filling the population with fright and revolt, but ultimately with shame for not being able to find ways to protest effectively, and being forced to accept one more humiliating hardship.

At the American Romanian Academy of Arts and Sciences (ARA) conference organized in Boulder in 1986, participants mentioned people being forced to cheat in order to survive in the wake of ever more punishing laws. A conference participant gave the following example: "They [the government] pass a law saying you can keep only three quarters of the plot on which you grow food to feed your family. But they do nothing about it so you keep using the entire plot. But they *do* know about it, and should you displease them in some way, they remind you of the law you broke. This is how everyone is made to feel guilty, this is how they control the population. To leave means not having to be humiliated, not having to be insulted anymore."

Given this situation in Romania, deprived of hope, I intensified my effort to grow roots here.

In 1988, forty years after our escape, I called my mother and proudly announced to her my victory, the fruit of decades of striving and struggling: "Mother, I have finally succeeded in accepting the fact that I will never again set foot on my native land, nor ever again see the world we left behind."

In the wisdom of her age, mother surprised me: "You can't say that, sweetie" she replied, "one never knows what the future holds . . ."

Then, suddenly, 1989 happened, and the entire edifice crumbled.

11
THE COLLAPSE OF THE SOVIET COMMUNIST EMPIRE

Wandering past a bookstore in Boulder's Crossroads Mall on a spring morning in 1989, I was thunderstruck by a title that sprang from among the covers on display:

THE GRAND FAILURE
THE BIRTH AND DEATH OF COMMUNISM IN THE TWENTIETH CENTURY
Zbigniew Brzezinski[58]

I could not believe my eyes—"The Death of Communism." What does it mean?

Could the Soviet Union no longer loom over our lives as the overwhelming, sorcerous power that darkened our horizon and cast the ominous shadow that weighed down my childhood, my youth, and much of my adulthood?

---

[58]Published by Charles Scribner's Sons, Macmillan Publishing Company, New York, 1989. Zbigniew Brzezinski was US President Jimmy Carter's National Security Advisor from 1977 to 1981.

As I grabbed the book and hungrily turned its pages, Brzezinski's text exposed, so clearly, what we refugees knew all along but could not find the words to convey it convincingly. "World War I . . . gave rise to movements [communism, fascism, Nazism] that wrapped the concept of social justice around a message of social hatred and that proclaimed organized state violence as the instrument of social redemption." Concepts difficult for us to impart because our voices had so long been drowned out by "the gut sympathy for communism," and "the international enthusiasm for Communism" that had spread to academics, to acquaintances, and even to our friends.

As to the "death of Communism in the twentieth century," could it truly be brought about as Brzezinski predicts—not from outside intervention, as I had been fervently hoping while struggling with public opinion, but from inside, as my mother foresaw three decades earlier?

A sequence of cascading, breath-suspending events across continents was reported shortly afterward in the media with stunning headlines:

Headline: **The Iron Curtain is Cut**

May 2, 1989: *"A soldier cut up the electrified fence on the Austrian-Hungarian border: The iron curtain is coming down."*

Was it really coming down? Or did this reconfirm instead its existence?

Headline: **Demonstrations in China**

May 17, 1989: *"A million Chinese students joined now by workers and professionals, even soldiers, are reported to be demonstrating in Tian An Men Square in Beijing, demanding democracy."*

May 23, 1989: *"Demonstrations in China continue."*

Hungarian troops dismantling the "Iron Curtain" 1989 (as illustrated in *Time* magazine, May 15, 1989).

I tried not to get too emotionally involved, not too hopeful, as I had for the Hungarian Revolution more than thirty years before.

May 30, 1989: *"Chinese fine arts students erected a Statue of Liberty in Tian An Men Square."*[59]

Statue of Liberty? My heart could not keep from leaping with joy.

June 3, 1989: *"The government troops are now shooting at the demonstrators."*

Dramatic views showed tanks rolling into the square, reminiscent of the crushed Hungarian Revolution. The photograph of the lone student facing down an oncoming armored car in the vastness of the square went viral. The following is from the account of a 20-year-old student at Quighua University, published in Hong Kong, then in the *New York Times* (June 12, 1989, p. A8).

---

[59]See Nicholas D. Kristof, "Beijing Reports Arrest of 11 Protesters." (Special to the *New York Times*, May 31, 1989).

> *The atmosphere was incredibly tense. For most of the students, this was the greatest danger they had ever faced. It would be a lie to say that we were not afraid, but we were mentally prepared and determined. Some students could not believe that the army really would use deadly force. But most of all, we were motivated by a powerful sense of purpose. We believed that it would be worth sacrificing our lives for the sake of progress and democracy in China.. . . the armored vehicles and additional forces that had been waiting on the square closed in on us, and we were completely surrounded by rows and rows of vehicles. . . .Thirty armored cars came crushing into the crowd. Some students died under the wheels. . . . Am I pessimistic? No, not at all. Because I have seen the will of the people. I have seen the hope of China. Some of my friends died. Even more are now bleeding. I am a survivor and I know how to live my life from now on. I will never forget the students who lost their lives. I also know for sure that all decent people in the world will understand and support us.*

The Chinese government's official line, issued by the Ministry of Truth, ("the big lie," as NBC anchor Tom Brokaw referred to it), was reported to be that no civilians had been killed, only troops were the victims. A strikingly open example of how Communist regimes have manipulated facts for the past 70 years.

The *New York Times* report of June 12, 1989, continued:

> *The movement is over. Maybe it can come back later, maybe there can be some underground organization, but essentially one is terrified into submission. Who can resist guns?*

One more attempt at freedom was crushed. Still, the event was energizing and hopeful because the "world" had witnessed it. No longer underground. No longer covered up. No longer explained away in seemingly rational terms. No longer denied or disbelieved.

Suddenly, the Communist world seemed to be morphing into a cauldron of bubbling demands, ferment, turmoil, restlessness with an avalanche of headlines: protests in Poland, Hungary, Siberia, the Ukraine, Lithuania, the Baltic Republics, the Moldavian Republic, East Germany, Bulgaria, Czechoslovakia, Moscow.

> June 6, 1989: *"Warsaw, Poland: Communists Concede Victory by Solidarity and Call for Coalition" [In the parliamentary elections, after the workers' trade union, founded 1980, demanded economic reforms and free elections.]"*[60]

> June 13, 1989: *"Hungarians Open Negotiations to Plan Multiparty Elections."*[61] [Until then, the Communist Party was the only party allowed.]

> July 18, 1989: *"Strike in Siberia Begins to Spread to the Ukraine."*

> August 23, 1989: *"35,000 Rally for Baltic Independence. . . Lithuania challenges 1940 annexation"* [to the Soviet Union].[62]

I was totally unprepared and felt almost faint with emotion at the ensuing news in print and on television:

> August 28, 1989: *"In the Moldavian Republic* [the former Romanian province annexed by Stalin at the beginning of the war] *the Romanian-speaking majority demand Romanian as official language."*

---

[60]*New York Times*, Tuesday, June 6, 1989.
[61]*New York Times*, Wednesday, June 14, 1989.
[62]*Denver Post*, Wednesday, August 23, 1989.

Out of the sea of Soviet darkness, these fellow Romanians could finally pierce to the light, their silenced voices heard at last, under the banner of the red, yellow and blue flag—our Romanian flag!—led by a man named Mircea, like my husband.

I could not get too excited. Too much time had passed, the outcomes were too uncertain. Any rejoicing on my part would have to wait until independence came.

Then the avalanche that took over all our awareness seemed unstoppable:

> October 8, 1989: *"Communists scrap party in Hungary . . . Nation to model new body on European socialism."*[63]

> October 23, 1989: *"300,000 Said to March in East German Protest*
> *. . . demanding democratic changes, including legalization of opposition movements, independent labor unions and separation of powers between the Communist Party and the state."*[64]

> October 24, 1989: *"Hungary becomes an official democracy . . . Thousands repudiate control by the Soviets."*[65]

> October 24, 1989: *"President Mikhail Gorbachev declared today that the Soviet Union has no moral or political right to interfere in the affairs of its East European neighbors."*[66]

No more crushing of Hungarian revolts? No more invasion of Czechoslovakia? I was very skeptical.

---

[63] *Denver Post*, Sunday, October 8, 1989.
[64] *New York Times*, Tuesday, October 24, 1989.
[65] *Denver Post*, Tuesday, October 24, 1989.
[66] *New York Times*, Thursday, October 24, 1989.

October 29, 1989: *"Czech protesters defy cops in defiant call for freedom. 10,000 fill Prague square despite official warnings."*[67]

October 30–31, 1989: *"Weekly Protests in Leipzig Draw 300,000 Marchers."*[68] *"Hundreds of thousands hold rallies in cities around the country."*[69]

November 4, 1989: *"The Lithuanian Parliament yesterday adopted enabling legislation that could lead to a referendum on independence from the Soviet Union."*[70] *"Bulgarians hold first protest since World War II."*[71]

November 8, 1989: *"Thousands protest in Moscow seeking an end to one-party rule in the Soviet Union."*[72]

November 8, 1989: *"Dissident activity was reported at other parades around the country* [for the 72nd anniversary of the Bolshevik Revolution], *principally in Kishinev, the capital of the Moldavian republic. Thousands there were said to have swarmed around a parade of tanks, demanding greater recognition of the rights of the republic's Rumanian-speaking majority"*[73]

Meanwhile in Germany,

---

[67]*Denver Post*, Sunday, October 29, 1989.
[68]*New York Times*, Tuesday October 31, 1989S.
[69]*Denver Post*, Friday, November 10, 1989.
[70]*Denver Post/International*, Saturday, November 4, 1989.
[71]*Denver Post*, Saturday, November 4, 1989.
[72]*New York Times*, Wednesday, November 8, 1989.
[73]*New York Times*, Wednesday, November 8, 1989.

November 4, 1989: *"More than 12,000 East Germans had swarmed across the border into Czechoslovakia in the three days since their government lifted a month-old ban on travel to the country, the only land East Germans may visit without prior permission."*[74]

November 5, 1989: *"Reeling from a dizzying week of political change, East Germany witnessed a gigantic pro-reform rally yesterday as 1 million East Germans took to the streets of the capital chanting 'Freedom! Freedom!' At the same time reports from Prague, Czechoslovakia, said East Germany had agreed to let its citizens leave for the West from Czechoslovakia simply by producing their internal identity documents."*[75]

The flood gates opened.

November 8, 1989: *"200 refugees an hour crossing Czechoslovakia to W. Germany. . . . The latest wave of East Germans swelled to more than 30,000 by last night, police officials said . . . the line of cars waiting to cross at the border was at least a mile and a half long."*[76]

November 8, 1989: *"East Germany's Cabinet Resigns, Bowing to Protest and Mass Flight."*[77]

November 9, 1989: *THE BERLIN WALL FALLS.*

---

[74]*Denver Post*, Saturday, November 4, 1989.
[75]*Denver Post*, Sunday, November 5, 1989.
[76]*Denver Post*, Wednesday, November 8, 1989.
[77]*New York Times*, Wednesday, November 8, 1989.

Delirium explodes as wave after wave of disbelieving East Germans approach the wall, checking that it is indeed safe to climb.

November 10, 1989: *"EAST GERMANY OPENS FRONTIER TO THE WEST FOR MIGRATION OR TRAVEL; THOUSANDS CROSS . . . CROWD IS ECSTATIC . . . Easterners Rush Across the Berlin Wall in a Mass Celebration."*[78]

All pandemonium breaks loose. By the tens of thousands, crowds from all over the city, East and West, rush to witness the tearing down of the hated barrier that for decades separated communities, neighborhoods, families, and ideologies. Germans from both sides of the wall scramble all over it, dance on it, smash it with hammers and axes to tear off pieces, shower it with champagne, set off fireworks, embrace each other singing with joy, and feast well into the night. And salute the memory of the hundreds who lost their lives attempting to scale the wall from East to West, to the freedom that lay beyond it.

For those who reach the other side of the wall, the contrast is almost overwhelming. From West Berlin:

[78]*New York Times*, Friday, November 10, 1989.

> November 12, 1989: *"One thin young East German stood paralyzed with incredulity before a colorful mountain of fruit and vegetables. "Oranges, Dirk! Oranges!" the youth exclaimed, nudging a companion in the ribs with the urgency of a miner who had struck gold."*[79]

A replay of our wonder, in Greece, almost 40 years earlier.

From Romania, though, no news other than "*Ceauşescu closes the border with Hungary.*"[80]

Even so, the dizzying changes in Eastern Europe bring a whirl of turmoil inside me. "I don't know whether to rejoice or to cry," I heard one Romanian comment.

Imagine the following scenario: Your house is broken into, your possessions stolen, and what is left is vandalized. Members of your family are beaten, some killed. You manage to escape and run for help only to find out that no one believes you: "That's not possible, it can't happen, it's not that bad, are you not letting your imagination run away? Did you go back to check it is really so? Do you have any proof? Maybe the intruders were trying to help. After all, your house was not in the best of shape to start with, it could have used some repairs. Perhaps if you had fed the intruders, if you had been kind to them." So you give up in anguish and despair.

Years later, the walls of the house crumble, some of those who were trapped inside come out, the others can throw away the intruders. At last. Do you rejoice? You breathe a sigh of relief, but your mouth is filled with the bitter taste of the needless ruin. Tired and drained, you go back and try to help rebuild the house.

That is how we felt about the whole oppressive grip.

---

[79] *Denver Post*, Sunday, November 12, 1989.

[80] *Time* Magazine, November 27, 1989.

The fall of the Berlin wall was followed in short order by Czechoslovakia's "Velvet Revolution," ushered in by massive (and peaceful) demonstrations led by acclaimed playwright and dissident Vaclav Havel.

November 27, 1989: *"Prague . . . Unshackled Czech Workers Declare Their Independence. . . . Like millions of workers throughout the nation, workers here walked off their jobs at noon in a two hour general strike demanding greater democracy and an end to the Communist Party's monopoly on power"*[81]

November 28, 1989: *"Factories, mills and mines shut down yesterday as crowds poured into the wintry streets. Bankers marched side by side with bricklayers, mathematicians with mechanics and dance teachers with crane operators in one great, big, delirious protest."*[82]

December 12, 1989: *"Czechs hail Communists' fall, settle down to choose a leader . . . Vaclav Havel, the playwright who was jailed for opposing communism and is now the driving force behind Civic Forum, the main opposition."*[83]

Then the news reports flash what was my dream for Romania:

December 12, 1989: *"From All Czechoslovakia, a Joyful Noise . . . Millions of Czech and Slovaks celebrated their country's dramatic political changes with five minutes of pandemonium at midday today. . . . Church bells pealed, sirens wailed and factory whistles hooted as people streamed into streets, squares and*

---

[81]*New York Times*, Tuesday, November 28, 1989.
[82]*Denver Post*, Tuesday, November 28, 1989.
[83]*Denver Post*, Tuesday, December 12, 1989.

> *boulevards. They tinkled bells and rattled keys, tea cups and beer mugs not only in Prague, but in cities from one end of the country to the other. . . Taxis, ambulances and even police cars joined in the joyous cacophony by hooting their horns to welcome the installation on Sunday of a cabinet that for the first time in 41 years puts the Communists in the minority"*[84]

"I never thought I would see this in my lifetime!" exclaimed a Romanian friend we met at a concert.

"I have the distinct feeling I am living after my death," "I feel I discover there *is* life after death!" Over and over again, the same overarching, unified exclamations spurt out, as if we are all compacted into a single being.

"I feel like Methuselah," muses Mircea.

Even if nothing happens in Romania, still I am gratified, relieved beyond words. There is a deep, underground elation, despite a feeling of numbness, as in a dream in which I am only a spectator and cannot affect the events. These are fantastic outcomes, they underline that hope should never be forsaken, despair should never be the victor.

My Boulder friend Magda whispers: "I pray for deliverance."

"Why whisper?" I question her.

"We never know who can hear" she cautions, "I worry for my father in Romania, for my family."

Ah, the tentacles of darkness are digging surreptitiously, even into the heart of the Free World!

Friday, December 22, 1989, 5:10 a.m. Mountain Time

It is pitch dark. We are deeply asleep. The telephone rings. Magda is on the line: "*Ceauşescu a căzut*!"

---

[84]*New York Times*, Tuesday, December 12, 1989.

Ceasuşescu is toppled!

Magda fills in details: "The minister of defense committed suicide, Corneliu Mănescu is forming a new government."

Her husband, Horia, comes on the line: "Did we wake you up?"

"It does not matter" I assure him, "We . . ."

"It *does* matter, we *want* to wake you up!!"

Still half asleep, I pass on the news to Mircea.

He jumps out of bed: "*Turn the TV on*!!"

Bucharest pops up. Bucharest, *direct* from Bucharest, unimaginable!!

People are on the streets, crowds are pressing as in a subway station when the train arrives, singing on top of their voices "*Deşteaptă-te Române*"[85] ("Wake up Romanian") and "*Hai să dăm mână cu mână ce-i cu inimă Română*"[86] ("Let's go hand in hand those with a Romanian heart").

Fired up by the full, harmonious voices vibrating from Bucharest in verses once forbidden, I decide to wake up the girls, even at this untimely hour. Singing at the top of my lungs, I wake up Adriana. She jumps from her upper bunk bed and runs to the TV. Then, still straining my voice with all my might, I reach Domnica downstairs. She is sunken in profound sleep. "Ceauşescu is gone!" I shout. The words pierce through the fog of her unawareness and then she also jumped up with none of the expected morning moaning, and races to the TV. Later I marvel that, contrary to custom, she rose without any coaxing: "You

---

[85]A patriotic song forbidden after the Soviet occupation of Romania [under the Communist government it imposed]. Freely translated, the main idea is: "Wake up, Romanian, from the sleep of death into which you sank under the cruel tyrants. Another fate go carve for yourself . . ."

[86]A patriotic song calling for unity and brotherhood among Romanians in the face of adversity.

don't realize, mother, that I spent all my life under Ceaușescu!" *She* did?

Shivering, for it is cold this December morning and we did not yet turn on the heat in the family room, we stay 15, 30, 45 minutes in front of the TV set, flipping from channel to channel. I call my parents in New York (my father answers), Mircea's brother calls us. Sandu Drosu calls with the news, we call Raluca in California before finally returning to bed for some sleep. But not for long. Julia Kintsch calls, then we call Nini in South Dakota; our kindred friends—the Frangopols, the Forseas, Maria Williams—all call us. It seems all Romanians are awake at this hour and the phones are buzzing.

Apparently, relatives in Europe were the first to pass on the news to our friends in Colorado: At 4 a.m. the Drosus's daughter called from Belgium. From Germany, Mihai Stan had called his sister Nini in South Dakota. Our friends from Paris called my parents. My high school friend Claude and her husband Bernard called from France, Mircea's friends called from Italy. It is all very emotional.

Domnica talks excitedly and screams with joy . . . Mircea and I hug quietly; he is on the verge of tears, I sob.

The stream of calls continues, this time from American friends. Bob Pois and also Cynthia Dunoyer. I call Lindsay Murdoch and Ann Scarboro. They both cry with me. I tell them how moving this is for us—not only the liberation of the country, but also the bonding with our American friends who helped us through this 40-year ordeal.

Susan Boucher calls, then Philippe Dunoyer to rejoice with us. Ann Scarboro stops by, and together we watch the streets of Bucharest fill with hundreds of thousands of people. I never thought I would see this moment. *Never*.

The entire day is spent on the phone, with European friends complaining later that for so long they were unable to get through to us. Only when we join the Scarboros for their Christmas sing-along at 5 p.m., after almost twelve hours on the phone, are we able to hang up.

We manage to pull together and intersperse the traditional English carols with the carols of our Romanian childhood, intertwining thus the two traditions that weave our new identity.

* * *

In Bucharest that Friday morning, December 22, 1989, Ceauşescu, the head of the government, had attempted to flee. For several days, rumors of demonstrations and shootings had pierced through a news blackout. In Yugoslavia, in Czechoslovakia, in Hungary, people with lit candles demonstrated in sympathy with the Romanians. But the fall of the Communist regime in Romania was not to be bloodless, as it was in neighboring countries.

The demise of Ceauşescu was brought on by a surge of demonstrators of all ages and all walks of life chanting "*Jos cu Ceauşescu!*" ("Down with Ceauşescu!") "*Jos cu dictatorul!*" ("Down with the dictator!") rolling from Timişoara in the west of the country on December 16 over the mountains, across the country, all the way to Bucharest in the east on December 22, swelling over the tanks and the bullets of the government forces.

The Ceauşescus, overwhelmed, attempted to flee. They were caught as they were about to climb into the helicopter that was to take them away. A few days later, mystery characters, whose voices alone were heard on the news, tried them summarily and executed them. Rumors identified these voices as those of Ion Iliescu, a former member of Ceauşescu's government, and Petre Roman, the son of another influential Communist. Though partly abated, the fighting still continued. Our hearts leapt with joy and emotion at the sight of the sea of Romanian tricolor flags with a hole in the middle where the Communist emblem had been torn out. The army now sided with the population, who had come out in the streets in droves, including children. Thirteen-year-old Luminiţa Boţoc was the first child known to be killed, in Timişoara.

Romanian tricolor flag with a hole in the middle where the Communist emblem had been torn out.

As I was to learn later, my cousin Emanuel had also come out in the streets of Bucharest with his 14-year-old son, Ion. For reasons that are still not clear to this day, there was a call to fight "terrorists." Who the terrorists were, no one knew. The feeling was that Iliescu attempted to frighten the population to get them on his side, even though he had been active in the Communist government and the people's sentiment was clearly anti-Communist. Eventually, Iliescu took control of the government. After weeks of day and night pro-democracy demonstrations that took root in University Square, with graffiti claiming solidarity with the Chinese students of Tian An Men Square, and chants of "down with neo-Communism!" Iliescu called on miners from the mountains of Transylvania, well over 100 miles from Bucharest, to club away the demonstrators. Those mines had been saturated by Ceauşescu with members of the "securitate" (Secret Police) after the miners had attempted a strike in the 1970s.

In 1991, two years after the downfall of the Communist regimes in Europe, the Soviet Union collapsed. Shortly thereafter, the Romanian province of Bessarabia, annexed by Stalin and renamed the Republic of Moldova, became independent. Slowly, the situation calmed down, borders were opened and, with intense emotion and trepidation, we now prepared to return, after a 43-year cut-off, to encounter what was left of our family and of our country as we had known it.

12

Rebirth after Four Decades of Soviet-Imposed Dictatorship and Separation

Forty-three years after we left Romania, on June 10, 1991, everything was ready for my return and, after months of upheaval, I drifted at last on the softness of this moment.

On a bright Colorado day, our friend Eileen drove us to the Denver airport. She was the first in a chain of warm, supportive companions who walked part of the way with us, sustaining us with their insights, their advice, and their empathy along this emotionally vulnerable journey. Mircea and Domnica left ahead on a Pan Am flight to New York's Kennedy airport, then on to Charles de Gaulle in Paris. Adriana sparkled with joy as she and I boarded the flight for Newark, where my aging father and ailing yet radiant mother awaited us at the gate. We exchanged last minute information about family and friends to contact, addresses, places to see and, half an hour before departure, the meaning of the moment, never before discussed with them, flooded me.

"Do you realize what this moment means?" I asked. My father listened in moved silence. My mother was visibly touched. "The first years after we left Romania, all I waited for, hoped for, prayed for was this moment" I reminisced.

"Yes, we too," nodded my mother.

"Then, from age 18 on, I did all I could to give it up."

"Yes," my mother joined in, "I also thought this moment would never happen. The revolution was a miracle." I hugged my mother, holding back my tears, then hugged my father who, for an instant, stopped worrying about helping us secure airplane seats, blankets, and overhead space.

On Our Way to Paris

Our four-day stopover in Paris on the way to Romania turned into a ritual as family after family of friends embraced us along the way, each inquiring about our progression toward the final goal. Among them was my cousin Dinu, whom I had not seen since he was four and I five playing under tables and chairs, and who, from our telephone conversation, felt as close to me as he did back then.

A major reconnection was with my childhood friend Anca, six years after our first reunion in Paris. Her mother Janine was visiting. Upon hearing me on the phone, "Aunt" Janine broke down and couldn't continue. It was the first time we heard each other's voices since I was a little girl.

At the Place d'Italie, Anca and I spent hours picking up where we left off earlier, in preparation for what I would find in Romania. At one point she commented on how much more I have remained true to my old self.

"You had many more responsibilities than I did," I observed, "escaping as an adult and needing to earn a livelihood for your family."

"No, it's the duplicity of life under the Communists that altered me most and gnawed at my integrity," she explained. "It was the constant fear of being denounced anonymously for any pretext, for a joke, for a criticism of the regime, or because you were claimed to have sabotaged

Anca and Ingrid at the Place d'Italie.

a technical project, or, in 1977–1982 when food was rationed, because you bought too great a quantity. With microphones installed everywhere, in your house, in your car, fear was permanent." She noted how spared we had been from the soul-wrenching compromises she and her brother Tudor had to make in order to live in that world. Tudor, who was denounced at a party for having danced rock (a symbol of the decadent Western culture), was given the choice of either becoming a party member[87] or facing prison and the end of a "normal" life. In addition to everything else, Tudor risked losing his architect's diploma, earned with six years of study and training, and consequently accepted becoming a Communist Party member.

[87]A Communist party member, since no other parties existed.

Even in Paris, the torment of past compromises, the constant concern of who collaborated, of who denounced, haunted the Romanian refugees. Some did not talk to each other, suspicious of who might be a "securist" (secret security agent) and spy on the exiled community.

Shortly before our departure, Mircea's friends, Jean and Simone Odiot, shared their fresh recollections from Simone's scientific trip to Moscow. She had just returned to Paris, overwhelmed by the depth of the suffering her fellow physicists in Russia revealed. One had just discovered that when his father had disappeared for years in his childhood, it was as an inmate in the Soviet Gulag. His father had never before mentioned his detention in Siberia.

The day before our June 25, 1991, flight to Bucharest, our friends Philippe and Nicole Playoust had treated us to dinner and to a mini tour along the Seine and its brightly lit monuments. The fireworks at Notre Dame were an intoxicating outburst of color and music against a centuries-old architectural masterpiece. The food, the setting, the mood, I suspected, could be in no greater contrast to what was awaiting us in Romania.

Landing in Bucharest

As we were landing in Bucharest, I expected soldiers, some sort of military presence, based on past travelers' reports. We barely saw any. What struck me immediately was an incredibly gray, dilapidated, tiny airport belonging to another age—another planet. The expression "run down" took on a life of its own. The fissures in the concrete leading to the entrance, the cracked glass doors, the old, tilted seats in the waiting room, the toilets with no light and no paper—everything drab and decaying, as if the place had fallen asleep fifty years ago and had never been touched or repaired, though squeaky with constant use.

I braced myself against the unpleasantness we might encounter. There was none. We were met by two local Romanian youths connected with the American Romanian Academy of Arts and Sciences

(ARA). This organization had been founded in exile to help us keep in touch with our culture, and now, for the first time, we were meeting in Romania. They guided us through passport control and to the retrieval of suitcases on a screeching conveyer that barely rolled, with baggage falling off right and left, next to a pile of what looked like abandoned luggage. We passed customs with no problem. "How much money do you have? More than a thousand dollars per person?"

"I wish!"

A large crowd was gathered outside the grimy glass doors. I tried to anticipate the features of my cousin Ileana—the last picture I had seen was of a six-year-old with braids. As we came out hesitantly, not knowing what to expect, we were accosted by cab drivers: "Taxi?"

Mircea spotted his childhood friend Puiu Constantineanu. They had shared a desk in high school. He came toward us.

Then I heard a hesitant question: "Griduţ?" That was my nickname, used only in my Romanian childhood. I looked at the lady who had spoken, her features nothing like the flat, round face I expected of Ileana. "I am Mihaela."

Mihaela! My cousin Emanuel's wife! Dear, devoted, overworked Mihaela, with her kind dark eyes and brave smile. With one of her four sons and a couple of Caritas[88] volunteers in tow, she was the one who came to meet us. Adriana, Domnica, and I jumped into the large Caritas van, and a cheerful youth named Cris drove us into the city, while Mircea followed in Puiu's car.

Bucharest's Otopeni Airport sits atop a hill. A wave of greenery slopes gently from the airport toward Bucharest, the lush trees parting for a wide avenue we followed into town, strikingly appealing. I was absorbing right and left the sight of the luminous cream-colored buildings, the peasants selling vegetables on the side of the road.

---

[88]Caritas is a Catholic charitable organization with which my cousin Emanuel was involved.

"That's about the only place where you will find fresh fruit," Mihaela commented.

Then large buildings in the Stalinist style I had heard of, and I shrank at the sight of them as we approached Bucharest proper, followed by the Arcul de Triumf[89] I remembered from my childhood. Then the tree-lined boulevard, Şoseaua Kisselef, so close to my childhood neighborhood, where my mother had taken me for walks and I had to stretch my hand to reach hers. Then came the city itself.

I looked and looked and looked, as Mihaela mentioned names that were all familiar—but what happened to the city? It was foreign, all gray and empty looking, even though the streets were populated. The buildings mirrored the airport: crumbing slabs of walls, blackened façades, dented balconies, streets in disrepair, sidewalks overgrown with grass and weeds—but above all, not a corner, not a spot that wasn't overtaken by this immense desolation. We stopped by Ileana's apartment, on Strada Speranţei, to pick up the keys to my cousin Daniela's apartment. My heart sank. No street could be more ill-named than Strada Speranţei (Street of Hope), for indeed all hope seemed to have been drained long ago. It was forlornness itself—not a trace of vegetation, no trees, no plants, no smile on the human shadows that moved about, no noise, no real life. This certainly must be a poor neighborhood, I thought, even though it used to be affluent.

"My first trip to Romania was an eye-opening experience," recalled Pulitzer Prize photojournalist nominee Michael Carroll about his 1990 trip to Romania a year earlier. "I was shocked to see a country so ravaged by years of neglect. The infrastructure was in a state of disrepair and the people were like shades on the street, afraid to look at you as you passed them. It was winter and the grayness of the season seemed to have passed into the soul of the people."[90]

---

[89]Triumphal Arch.

[90]*Gândacul de Colorado*, April 2011, no.111, p. 9.

"*Allucinante*" ("Hallucinating"), exclaimed a passing Italian visitor, staring, amidst an overpowering stench, at a block of newer buildings that were decaying at an accelerated rate. Not a dream, not a nightmare, but a distortion of reality so grotesque it could not be real.

Would Daniela's apartment where we were to stay on Dr. Pasteur Street, one of Bucharest's best neighborhoods, be in better shape? It was situated in the "doctors' neighborhood," so-called because its streets were named for eminent physicians, including my great-great-grandfather, Dr. Iatropol.

Hers was an old-style, welcoming neighborhood. Yet the same appearance of a ghost town pervaded. We arrived at #37, where, the stairway to the second floor was dark, the wooden floors inside the apartment tarnished with years of neglect, the rooms dimly lit, the bathroom and the kitchen at least 50 years ancient. And there was the smile of Simona, the bright young woman who was living in the apartment and cheerfully made room for us, acting as if this state of desperation was normal.

As I settled the girls for the night on the living room sofas, Adriana's tears rolled down her cheeks: "Mommy, I realize this city must have been so beautiful, one of the most beautiful I have ever seen, but what happened to it? Will it ever be normal again?"

Domnica had maintained her cheer throughout the airport: "Oh, it's not that bad. . . . It's just how one looks at it!" But now her face was drawn in pallor. "This is so sad, so sad. Will we be able to return home sooner if we want to?"

I tried to divert her attention: "We'll work to help, to rebuild the country. We'll do our best to bring some relief."

"But I wouldn't even know where to start!" she countered.

"Tomorrow you'll go with your cousin Andrei to Caritas. You will see what goods they received from abroad and you'll help distribute them to those in need. We'll take it from there."

First Contact with Tudor

The next morning the telephone rang. It was Ileana: "Tudor has called several times already. He is raring to see you, he is ready to come over right now but does not dare call you. Is it all right if he calls?"

All right? Tudor, that fascinating presence in my childhood. Tudor, three years my senior, who knew everything and could do anything, especially drawings that amazed the adults. Tudor, the one I thought of, dreamt of throughout prison and in the yard at Zrenianin, almost willing its gate to open and let in my friends Tudor and Anca. Tudor, who was in my thoughts throughout my adolescence in New York City or in the back of the car as we drove to Long Island for the weekend. I would make myself dizzy trying to imagine our first encounter after the fall of the Communist regime.

But I had grown up since and matured, and I was now married to a wonderful man who also "knows everything," at least in the scientific fields that absorb me, with also a marked gift for sketching—a caring companion with whom I can share all my experiences, the father of my two daughters. Tudor himself was married (twice), had two daughters, and even though I wrote him a letter of vibrant memories when he turned 50 and he responded in kind, there was nothing between us but our childhood memories.

And now, his impatience to see me.

I dialed his number immediately and he answered. I laughed incredulously. To hear his voice seemed so absolutely implausible.

"When can I come over?"

"Any time, right away if you wish." It was 10:00 a.m. "How's 10:30?"

I had barely finished combing my hair and getting ready when, at 10:30 a.m. sharp, the doorbell rang. It was the downstairs bell. I raced down the steps, but no one was at the entrance door to the building, nor at the gate to the street. I went back upstairs, looked from the balcony, and saw no one on the street. I rushed back down and was about to walk into the street when a lean man dressed casually in black slacks and a black open shirt, approached the gate hesitantly, a bouquet of flowers in his hand.

"You will not recognize him; he has aged terribly" his sister Anca had warned me in France. "He has lost all his hair."

What I saw was a youthful Yul Brynner, the masculine star of *The King and I*, who made a shaved head seem sexy. He looked very much as I remembered his father, with Anca's mouth and young Tudor's mischievous gleam in his eyes. But the gleam was less playful and more sarcastic.

"Tudor?" I inquired.

He didn't seem to know what to say or do. I threw my arms around his neck and hugged him. He seemed to feel awkward.

I told him he looked like his father, he said he had not been sure which was the entrance to the house. I led him upstairs. Mircea and the girls were there, and no one was very talkative. The girls eyed him with curiosity, Mircea with friendly reserve. We were all in the kitchen—he had accepted a cup of hot chocolate (American cocoa with powdered milk, brought from Boulder)—and I was trying to boil the milk and find a vase for his flowers and keep the conversation up all at the same time. The milk was sticking to the pot. The girls were all absorbed by Tudor. "Come, people, help me!" I exclaimed and regretted it immediately.

Finally, we sat in the living room, on the two sofas. The conversation was mainly three-way, Mircea, Tudor, and I, with the girls absorbing every word. I don't remember what we said except that the flow was not easy and I kept on trying to make him out. Here was this black-clad, intimidating Yul Brynner in front of me but also the mischievous, laughing young boy who had so impressed me, and yes, intimidated me, in my childhood—which was which, and who was this man?

After exchanging some childhood recollections and some details of our present life, he left at about noon, with the anticipation of more meetings in the days to follow. The meaty part of our encounter was to occur downstairs. We spent a good bit of time talking at the gate, alone, about his father, about his father's insistence that Tudor's two sisters leave Romania, even if it meant that Anca had to escape, while at the same time restraining Tudor from doing the same. His father said Tudor should wait for a good, safe way to leave the country and he would see to it that he would find this occasion. But then his father died and it was too late. His father had guided his children with an iron hand.

"I matured only when Anca left home," he confessed, "and so did she. Until then, my father did everything for us."

I found him frail now under a cynical demeanor. He seemed lost in this bleakness and making do bravely.

"I could have stayed in France when I visited last year. But every time I thought about it, there were things that held me back. I have a home here that I have created over the years to my taste and I love it. I have a family."

When I returned to the apartment, the girls were swooning. "He's a stud!"

"A stud? Why on earth?"

"He is so shy," explained Domnica, "And I love the way you two interact."

"And he's so nice too, and he seems to like you so much, the way he looks at you," added Adriana.

The strong bond seemed to have endured, beneath the torn roots, the rubble, the muck stacked over the years. Yet how much was it a bond with me and how much the lure of the West that has eluded him?

We were to meet again several days later.

Slipping into Daily Life in Bucharest

The first few days in Bucharest were oppressive. The ragged face of the city, disfigured by disrepair, stared me in the eye—the graphic expression of the pain that had gripped me for the past forty years.

Even at night, despite the cloak of darkness, the weight of this total degradation pressed down on my chest and I thought I knew what a heart attack felt like. Those who recoiled at the thought of returning and witnessing the country in its present state may have had a point.

As darkness settled one evening, I opened the window to distract our daughters from this general oppression and called out to them: “Come, come smell the linden trees, the warm, full aroma of the linden trees! And look at the moon! That’s how it appeared from the balcony of our house on Strada Paris[91] when my mother sang *Luna ştiiiie, dar nu spuuune, multe taine diiin trecut* (The moon knows, but will not tell, many secrets from the past), enticing me to want to become an astronomer and find out its secrets.”

At lunch the next day, we ate near the once-elegant Athénée Palace Hotel, close to the former Royal Palace. There, in November 1945, while Soviet tanks were roaming the streets of Bucharest, tens of thousands of young people, including Mircea, filled Piaţa Regală, the vast square in front of the Royal Palace, chanting their support of young King Michael on his name day.[92] Suddenly, shots were fired from the rooftop of the nearby Ministry of Home Affairs (later the headquarters of the Central Committee of the Communist Party from whose balcony Ceauşescu spoke on the fateful December 1989 day when he was booed and attempted to escape). Nineteen-year-old Mircea ran for cover; demonstrators were killed, students were arrested. Our friend Andrei Doneaud, 17 at the time, was imprisoned in the subterranean cells of the sinister Fort Jilava.

The food at the restaurant was almost unpalatable. That evening we dined on dried soup and raisins we had brought from Boulder, having been forewarned of the bleak situation in the country. Adriana, her face

[91]Taken over by the Communist government, I believe in 1951, without any compensation.

[92]The feast of St Michael, November 8, 1946.

tense and scared, wondered if we would die of hunger. I reassured her as best I could, remembering that I had survived in prison on much less.

The next day, in search of food, I went exploring the neighborhood market at the end of our street: a large hall, flooded with sunlight, spacious, inviting—and empty but for a stack of tomatoes piled on a large table in the middle of the room and, lined on a shelf by the wall, a few bottles of soda manufactured by an American company. That was the *aprozar*, the state-owned fruit and vegetable store, and those were the only fruits and vegetables to be found there. But I knew peasants were selling fresh produce, so I searched for them outside. On neat, covered, brick stalls, they had spread potatoes, onions, cucumbers, squash, radishes, some herbs—all at prices excessive for a local population earning, on average, $100 a month at best.[93]

To get a feel for the present situation, I struck a conversation with some of the peasants. At first, they were reticent. But after they learned we came from the United States and wanted to find out what their situation was now, they gradually opened up. They said they had still not received land and they did not know how much of the crop planted on the strip of land the state allotted to them they would be able to keep. The uncertainty was made worse by prices that had greatly increased, almost tripled.

"Are you hopeful that the situation will improve?" I asked a woman.

"Not much," she replied. "Under Ceaușescu at least there was some order. There was someone to fear. Now there is no one to fear. Something has to happen."

"Will the peasants revolt?"

"No way. All we know is hard work and putting up with things. We won't revolt. Someone has to produce food."

---

[93]50 lei for a kg of tomatoes represented roughly 46 cents per pound at the 1991 exchange rate of 60 lei per US dollar. For someone earning $100 a month, this was a significant expense.

Ramiro Sofronie, a professor of civil engineering who came to pick up a letter from Daniela, summed it up in a diverging point of view: "Things are much better now."

"Better?"

"Spiritually. We can speak up, take initiatives, move freely. Things are better spiritually, worse materially."

The "worse materially" aspect hit us at the butcher's next door. I thought Romania was better off than the Soviet Union. Yet what we found here struck us as a replica of the Moscow market we had seen on television: empty shelves lining whitewashed walls. What television could not convey was the pungent, nauseating, overpowering stench. It came from a pile of white, shiny fat left on a table in the middle of the room. A sign read: "pork meat." No trace of meat. With hungry children at home, I could feel the panic the locals must experience.

"You went too late," explained Simona. "People who want meat line up at 6 in the morning to wait for the 8 o'clock truck. That's when the better meat is to be found. But I have to go to work at 7:30, so I cannot wait in line." She gets her food from her mother, who lives in the countryside.

In the evening the girls' minds worked furiously: "I want to leave earlier. I feel like dying if I stay here any longer," from Adriana, followed by Domnica: "I wish I had been here under Ceausescu."

"But, Domnica, you can barely stand it now!"

"Just for a day . . . Mom, do people believe you when you explain what this is like here? I heard about it all my life and I could never have imagined this. I could never understand this."

The first relief occurred during the opening ceremony for the American Romanian Academy of Arts and Sciences conference inside the jewel-like Ateneu Concert Hall. So resplendent in marble, gold leaves, frescoes, and exquisite nineteenth-century decor that we could have been in Paris or in Rome. It had escaped the dilapidation that screamed on the outside. For two hours, we could forget and breathe more freely.

The opening notes of an Enescu rhapsody announced the beginning of the concert just as Ghizi, freshly arrived by overnight train from Miercurea Ciuc in central Transylvania appeared, arms overflowing with peonies from her garden. Ghizi's mother, Roji, had helped my mother care for me. They were both as devoted to us as the most loving of family members. I could not greet her warmly enough. The celebrated strains reunited us in silent concentration. While Ghizi recollected about listening to this rhapsody with her mother, I was grabbed by a vision from the past: to that piece and with intense longing, at age 16, I had choreographed in my mind's eye a radiant pastoral dance on the open fields of a free Romania, never suspecting I would hear these same strains as a middle-aged adult together with Ghizi and my own young family, in an indeed free Romania.

Sharing, at Last, Our Experiences with My Countrymen

ARA lectures, interviews, receptions absorbed us almost entirely for several days, culminating, for me, in the feverishly anticipated moment when, after emerging from a double odyssey, captivity and exile, I could at last go back and share with a Romanian audience in a free Romania the account of our escape to the West. The girls were in the room, bright with anticipation and cheerfully glancing at me from time to time. My heart leapt with joy and gratitude when Mircea entered the overcrowded classroom, its walls lined with young people. I was tensely awaiting my turn when, just as I was about to begin, Ladis Kristof[94] stepped in: "I came to hear your presentation." He had been in prison with us at Kovačica—he a young man, I a child. I was especially moved.

[94]Father of Pulitzer-prize winning *New York Times* columnist Nicholas Kristof.

After an improvised introduction to fit into the train of thought of the session, I relaxed, found my pace and my message flowed easily, impassioned, from my inner well. I ended on a vibrant note about the need to acknowledge the devastation wrought by the Communist regime in order to heal as a nation and move forward. The audience responded warmly. As the questions were cut short for lack of time and the next speaker was introduced, we all four left the packed room.

Tudor was outside, waiting. "Why didn't you tell me you were making a presentation? I would have loved to hear you," he asked in as subdued a tone as possible. "I thought I did. . . ." The girls (who shamelessly listened to my conversations) assured me I didn't. I offered to have him listen to the recording Mircea made and he immediately accepted.

At lunch we were joined by two other congress participants, who approached me about my experience. The conversation became a balancing act between a general interaction with the two attendees and a personal exchange with Tudor who was eagerly inquiring—although repeatedly interrupted—about our escape from Yugoslavia.

At about 3:30 p.m. we walked Tudor to his car. He was leaving Bucharest the next day on business and then to Constanţa on the shores of the Black Sea to pick up his wife and daughter. We arranged to see them the next week.

During the rest of the ARA conference, the girls slumped in the apartment, Adriana displaying symptoms of "existential fatigue" as described in one of the ARA lectures. It had been exhibited by the peasants whom Ceauşescu had forcefully transplanted into the city in hastily erected buildings, several stories high with no indoor plumbing: fright, fatigue, depression.

Embracing Life in Bucharest

Adriana's persistent fear of hunger was allayed as we ate at receptions, at friend's houses and, regularly, at the "cantina," the university lunchroom. There, they served an excellent three course meal for under 100 lei, or 50 cents at the black market rates we obtained from youths who openly bought dollars at Piaţa Amzei.

"Why do you want dollars?" I inquired of one of them.

"To emigrate."

"Where?"

"To Australia."

I quickly turned my head to hide my emotion. Australia was one of the lands advertised on posters at the refugee center in Athens when we reached Greece, a place where immigrants could settle. In 1950, before the age of air travel, it felt as remote as the moon, a place of no return. These young people had obviously no hope for their future in Romania.

Despite the culinary prowess displayed there, the fare at the "cantina" was basically a variation of pork and potatoes, cabbage and tomatoes. After three weeks of this regimen, the lunch offered on the Fourth of July in the vast gardens of the palatial residence of the US Ambassador on the posh Şoseaua Kiseleff, was to strike us as positively succulent: hot dogs and Pepsi! Domnica and Adriana were to bloom in this surrounding—everywhere US flags and Marines.

Now, back in our kitchen, the girls were laughing. With the routine, the cantina felt like home in its airy, green setting with the friendly, extra-efficient waitresses. In due time, in visits to friends and in different markets, we were to discover foods that would make our mouths water in longing when we returned to the States: the sweetest, most succulent tomatoes we were ever to sink our teeth into; the texture and taste of Caşcaval, the sheep cheese recalling the Italian "caciocavallo" we had never discovered in the States; the thirst-quenching mineral waters such as Borsec and Bucovina; the lusciousness of the prize-winning Romanian wines, Cotnari, Fetească, Murfatlar.

Domnica said she felt almost as if she were born here. I felt nourished by the soil, the air, the moisture, the people all around. I saw less of the decay and more of the exquisite motifs decorating the windows, the columns, and the lintels below the roofs.

As we slipped into the local fold, the focus changed. We mingled on the streets with the people of Bucharest, starting conversations with strangers with the ease of old acquaintances. Adriana and Domnica marveled at the faces of the children, recognizing their own features: "They look like us!"

At Home in a Lunar Landscape

To reconnect with the city, I wandered alone on a long, haphazard walk, wet in the rain, and found myself heading toward Grădina Icoanei,[95] a name engraved in my subconscious memory, a name with a far, faraway resonance. Yet the area was so gray and barren and out of place, not urban and not countryside either, as strange as a moonscape. I was seized by the sensation that I stepped on lunar land. Nothing terrestrial here. Yet, somehow, I felt as deeply rooted in it as if it were my mother's bosom. I had panicked when Jean left us at Orly. But here, in this totally alien surrounding, all fear had left me. Here, I was enfolded in the security of my childhood. Here, nothing could go wrong.

At night, we would fall asleep to the barking orchestra of the city's dogs. In the morning we would wake up to the faraway, appeasing rhythms of my Bucharest childhood: the cooing of the doves.

Stumbling upon the Past under the Linden Trees

Mircea and I strolled arm-in-arm in our neighborhood one evening, under an umbrella of leaves, taking in the silhouettes of the houses in the penumbra of the trees: the intimate arches, the diminutive columns, the arabesques under the windows, the typical Romanian architecture

[95] A small park in the center of Bucharest.

imbued in my soul—my childhood suddenly no longer lost. It is here under our footsteps, in our nostrils, in the familiar lushness of the air, in the sweet, penetrating aroma of the linden trees, as I had encountered nowhere else with this pungent intensity. As in a fairy tale, I am transported to my childhood world. Through the layers of time I am welded, once again, to my first years, to my innermost me. I *did* go back to the Romania I left after all!

Our daughters cannot see this Bucharest. For them, I suspect, it is dark and decrepit, beautiful only in its poignantly lost past. But Mircea, who was nineteen when he left, can partake in it with me. Perhaps he, too, can feel what I feel. "Perhaps this is why I married you, for this moment," I surmise. He laughs.

Further Reconnections Feed My Soul

While waiting for my Aunt Helga and Uncle Horia to return from their visit to their son Adrian in Germany, we had a chance to renew more contacts.

On the Street of Despair (as I thought of the "Strada Speranţei"), the apartment of Ileana and her mother Clementina opened up on an oasis of elegant old-time furnishings and a vision of a world now past. Ileana pointed to the tall wardrobe they had pushed against the windows as protection from stray bullets flying in from the street fighting that erupted in December 1989 after Ceauşescu's capture and execution. It had been a time of intense fright for them, and of gnawing suspense for us as we watched it on the TV screen of our safe home in Boulder. It still felt raw in Bucharest.

My cousin Rucky, Mihai's sister, shared a small apartment with their father, my Uncle Valter, in the center of the city, on Vasile Lascăr Street. Stouter and wearier than when I knew him—as worn down now as the city's buildings—my uncle greeted us with the same humorous twinkle in his eyes I remembered from my childhood. As for 49-year-old Rucky, now an architect and painter of icons, she cut the slender and sprightly silhouette of a teenage ballerina. Delicate and quiet, Rucky's sensitivity balanced the self-assurance Ileana had maintained since early childhood, when she had so impressed me.

Rucky and Ileana fed my soul with recollections of my beloved grandfather and of our young, athletic Uncle Eugen, Clementina's younger brother, who had dazzled our childhood with rides on his motorcycle and with his prominent right biceps that moved with a life of its own.

Two years my senior, this eminently practical and world savvy Ileana amazed me with her reaction upon seeing the map of Bucharest we had brought from the States: "Where did you get this? The city's map is nowhere to be found here!!"

Amazement for amazement, I could not believe the reply I received in a shop that advertised copy-making when I asked how long it would take to replicate the map we had brought: "A week" was the answer. *A*

My cousins Mihaela, Ileana, and Rucky. Mihaela, born after we escaped from Romania, is the daughter of Uncle Eugen. I was to meet her on a later trip.

week? A copy machine back home would accomplish the task in a matter of seconds! "Of course," was the reply. "We must photograph the document, develop the film, then make a print."[96]

Very different proved to be the recollections evoked by my mother's lifelong friend, Sanda Zaharia. She arrived at our apartment for 5 o'clock tea. Beneath her expression, which now evinced years of trials and deprivation, I detected the luminous freshness of mien captured in my parents' wedding pictures. She mentioned the several years in a row when they had had no meat and how her eyes welled up when her son finally found, in the countryside, pork meat that he brought home, at a time when milk, eggs, fish, fruit, and vegetables were also lacking.

Tears also flowed, she recollected, the first time water ran from the faucet. For months and years, they were obliged to collect water drop by drop at night. The last six years under Ceauşescu had been the worst.

At first, when Ceauşescu fell, she had exploded with optimism and relief. Now, talking about the present situation, she apologized for the sadness of the subject. Overall, she was very pessimistic. She kept on looking at her watch so as not to overstay, I kept on encouraging her to remain. When she left, it was reluctantly . . . after so many years.

Much more cheerful was the exceptional musical reconnection when we gathered at the home of Viorica and Vlad Voiculescu, both physicians and the Fotino family's most stalwart friends. There, we were joined by Mircea's petite, delicate, unassuming, exquisitely sensitive, and gifted cousin, pianist Maria ("Cuca") Fotino. At Mircea's initiative, some of her recordings he obtained from the Romanian Broadcasting Corporation were reissued in 2005 under the British Pearl label and the title "The Art of Maria Fotino." In no time they elicited

---

[96]Just a few years later, maps were to be found everywhere and, most amazingly, *online*!—in color, with all the information we could wish for, including updated bus and train schedules, previously difficult to obtain. Ubiquitous were also the ATMs—no need to have recourse to emigrating young people to exchange our dollars for the local currency.

enthusiastic Western reviews: "One of the finest pianists and teachers in the middle decades of the twentieth century";[97] "a model of interpretive nuance," "refreshing natural simplicity," and "ripe romanticism";[98] "capable of exuberant energy and joy";[99] "the most distinguished pianist of her generation in Romania."[100] Sitting at the piano next to 78-year-old Cuca, 19-year-old Domnica, who had been considering becoming a pianist before aiming for medical school, absorbed the distilled experience and finesse Cuca was so gently and modestly conveying. A most precious interaction between generations.

Royal Castle and Family Villa at Sinaia in the Carpathians

The musical thread was pursued into the Carpathian Mountains with Mircea's high school classmate and lifelong friend, Puiu Constantineanu, who had met us at the airport. As a practicing physician, Puiu had given up promising promotions in his career rather than accept, as pressured by the Communist Party, to become a party member. He compensated for the loss by immersing himself in literature, writing, and music at his home.

In a step back in time to Mircea's childhood, Puiu drove us to the resort town of Sinaia, 120 km north of Bucharest, where Mircea, his parents, and his older brother Şerban had vacationed in summer in Villa Marcella throughout the years. It is there that Carol I, Romania's first king, who had been invited to come from Germany when he was Prince Karl of Hohenzollern to rule the recently liberated and united Romanian principalities of Moldavia and Wallachia,[101] had built the Peleş

[97]Blair Sanderson's review of the Pearl label CD : "Maria Fotino Performs Mozart, Scarlatti, Chopin, Schumann, Enescu."

[98]Alan Becker, "American Record Guide," vol. 68, no. 6, Nov 2005, p. 299.

[99]Benjamin Ivry, "International Piano Magazine," Sept/Oct 2005.

[100]Lance G. Hill, Editor-in Chief, The Classical Musical Guide Forums, Sept 25, 2006.

[101]Carol I ruled from 1866 to 1881 as prince, from 1881 to 1914 as king.

Castle we were going to visit. The drive on serpentine mountain roads along picturesque hamlets was an enthralling passage to another realm.

As soon as we passed Breaza and reached Posada, the hamlets transformed into a collection of tidy, freshly painted, daintily decorated homes, flowers blooming everywhere—what a contrast with Bucharest! "That's because of the relative wealth of the mountain people, as forced collectivization was not practicable in the mountainous areas" explained Simona later, when she treated us to a bunch of succulent, fresh young carrots ("I could not find any fruit," she explained). We first reached the monastery at Sinaia, gleaming in its gold, brick, and blue hues—a jewel of balance and poetry. The diminutive older monastery emerged: white, sober, and moving in the stillness of its setting.

Peleş Castle

Peleş Castle, built over several decades from the end of the nineteenth to the beginning of the twentieth century, had us agasp: on top of a hill rising amidst lush greenery with freshly piled haystacks at its base, it looked like a sweet, idyllic Hansel and Gretel construction. Inside, its Florentine, French, Mooresque, and Turkish rooms intensified the feeling of a storybook apparition, bewildering in the otherwise grim state of affairs.

In Sinaia proper, on Bulevardul Carol I, Villa Marcella stood in a sore state. It was Mircea's family mountain residence, named for his mother, and now occupied by three families to whom the state sold it after having nationalized it in 1951 without any compensation to his family. Sad, too, was the state of Villa Luminiş in the Cumpătul neighborhood, the retreat of Romania's celebrated musician and composer George Enescu (1881–1955), a significant presence in the life of Mircea's family.

George Enescu.

A child prodigy, Enescu had graduated from the Vienna Conservatory with highest honors and a silver medal when he was not yet thirteen. During his lifetime, he would be celebrated for his exquisite violin virtuosity and his outstanding gift as conductor. Enescu is now famed for his Romanian Rhapsodies heard periodically on the radio and, among music lovers, for his opera "Oedipe," for his suites for violin and piano and presently for the international George Enescu Festival held every other year in Bucharest and various other Romanian cities. Back in 1949 at Enescu's musical evenings in Villa Luminiş, Cuca, who was Enescu's favorite interpreter for his piano compositions, would sometimes perform with him, while teenage Mircea turned pages and absorbed the events with the intensity of one tempted by a career as a violinist before opting to devote himself to science.

On our return to Bucharest, after passing Buşteni, the small mountain resort where mother had taken me for a respite of fresh air in my early childhood while my father was away on business trips, the Caraiman Peak suddenly appeared like a huge curtain hanging from the sky above,[102] taking our breath away.

Finding Out about Uncle Horia's Imprisonment

Back in Bucharest, I prepared with trepidation for our long-awaited meeting with my father's younger sister Helga and her husband Horia. When we first landed in Romania ten days prior, Uncle Horia and Aunt Helga were in Germany visiting their son Adrian. (Uncle Horia didn't get to know Adrian until he was 16 years old, when Uncle Horia was released from prison.) They returned to Bucharest just in time to meet us before our departure.

Aunt Helga had struggled to raise her two sons on a salary equivalent to a quarter of her father's pension, always fearing to lose her job were it to be discovered she was not divorced, but rather the wife of a political prisoner. The packages of food, clothing, fabric, and medications my father sent regularly to my grandfather—some to be sold, others to be used by them—helped supplement their needs while Uncle Horia was in prison, perhaps not even alive as far as she knew.

How did Uncle Horia survive more than 16 years in prison in almost total isolation from his family and remain whole in mind and in soul? He was now active as a spiritual adviser for priests, exhibiting his paintings, writing letters full of humor. Other prisoners, after 6 or 7 years of incarceration, returned as broken men, staring their life away at a television set or a wall—living human vegetables. What was my

---

[102]Caraiman Peak stands at 2,260 m, or roughly 7,400 ft. The altitude is not impressive, but its apparition is startling.

uncle's amazing secret? Religion would not have been a satisfactory explanation for me. To understand the answer to this puzzle was one of my main aims on this trip.

It took us about 30 minutes or more to discover, by taxi, the new housing developments where they lived on the outskirts of Bucharest. They were so run down that the rest of Bucharest almost seemed to be in good shape. The overwhelming stench made the air difficult to breath. "Hallucinating" is what the Italian tourist exclaimed upon coming to this same neighborhood. After a persistent search, we found the right building, the right entrance, and decided to entrust our lives to the rickety elevator that pulled us up to the fifth floor.

My aunt opened the door and we entered another world. There was not the slightest intimation of the disaster area they inhabited. Aunt Helga bore a striking resemblance to my father—his facial features, his gray hair, and the same strong, warm, all-enveloping hug. Her face radiated the gentle, caring soul I had sensed in her letters.

Behind her came my uncle. I recognized him immediately from the clean, sharp, fine features I remembered from my childhood. But his sight was clearly altered: he had lost an eye in prison in a workshop accident. He came closer. He did not smile but stared intently into my face with a searching gaze, as if to penetrate through the layers that had been deposited over the years and get through to the expression of the little girl he had once known. It was the most intense and poignant gaze, a deeply moving expression of interest, at once evincing true caring and acknowledging the pain of the loss inflicted by a separation that was most unnatural and lasted, oh, so many, many years.

As we sat down, after he commented on the revolution and the new situation in the country, I asked him point blank: "What was prison like for you?"

The swift change in his expression and his knowing smile clearly conveyed the message: "See? I *knew,* I just *knew* she would ask me about prison!"

Then without much ado, he proceeded to tell me.

Before being imprisoned, my uncle had converted to Catholicism under the influence of a saintly spiritual guide, Monsignor Ghika. He then offered his life to God. "My arrest was a sure sign that God had accepted my life, for He put it to use where it was most needed—in prison."

To give us a sense of the conditions there, he walked us through one specific day: the prisoners would wake up, empty their buckets, then sit on the edge of the bed in the cell for the rest of the day. He wanted to practice a Morse alphabet with his fingers. Through the peephole a guard saw him. "What are you doing?" he shouted. "I'm looking at my hands," my uncle answered. "Put your hands down!" the guard ordered.

Despite this vigilance, my uncle succeeded in communicating with prisoners from other cells by tapping messages in the Morse alphabet or by knotting them on a thread pulled out of his towel. When they emptied their buckets, he would drop the thread where other prisoners could pick it up. He thus passed on the content of a book he had composed in the early days when conditions were less dire, describing his vision of the world and his religious beliefs. Earlier in their incarceration, a cellmate, under his dictation, had scratched the words on the walls of the cell, as no pencil and paper were allowed. (When they were arrested, the prisoners were permitted no personal belongings; even a handkerchief was violently taken away from a man with a cold who was using it to blow his nose.)

Eventually, guards spotted the letters on the wall and erased them. By then, though, both my uncle and his companion had memorized the book,[103] three-days' worth of recitation.

But, my uncle wondered, how to reach the most wretched of the prisoners?

---

[103]Published after his liberation and the fall of Ceauşescu's regime under the title *Manualul Omului Politic Creştin* (Editura Crater, Bucureşti, 1995, ISBN 973-9029-16-7). (Title translation:is *Manual of the Christian Political Man.*)

The answer came when he was confined to one of the harshest cells, below ground, flooded with water except for a small dry island in the middle of the floor. There, the inmates, stripped to their shorts in the freezing winter temperatures, took turns sleeping for two hours curled under a sheep's fur, while the rest walked round and round, nonstop, to keep the blood circulating. In this setting, my uncle shared his message of faith, trust, and hope.

No contact with family was allowed, with one exception: prisoners who volunteered to work in the shop a certain number of extra hours a day would be allowed to receive a letter from their family. Prisoners could receive a package for working longer hours; for still longer hours they could receive the unthinkable—a visit. To his fellow prisoners' surprise, my uncle never volunteered. As an old hand in the system, he knew the promises would not be kept, as indeed they were not.

Uncle Horia touched lightly on some of the tortures meted out, such as being forced to stand for days in a very confined space in which a man could not sit, until his ankles swelled to the size of a grapefruit. He commented on hunger: "You think you know what hunger feels like, but you don't. It's not what you think; it's when every cell in your body, every strand of hair, the tip of every nail screams for food." The prisoners were so altered by this treatment that, were they separated for, say, a couple of years, upon meeting again in some other prison they would not recognize each other. (My uncle was incarcerated in at least seven different prisons.)[104]

What, then, was the secret of his survival, both physical and emotional? At last I understood. The secret was an aim higher than himself, an aim that he could pursue even—or especially—in prison. An aim that gave meaning to his suffering. Incarceration allowed him to reach those in pain and to help them. While in prison, Uncle Horia, by many

---

[104]According to my cousin Emanuel and his wife Mihaela, these are Jilava, Arsenal, Mărgineni, Ocnele Mari, Aiud, Periprava, and Gherla prisons.

accounts, brought hope to the most dejected. One prisoner, upon his release, confided that Horia's words and example saved his life when he was about to commit suicide. Everything that happened to Uncle Horia, no matter how cruel—torture, hunger, isolation from family and friends and from the outside world, the loss of an eye—had a meaning, everything could be turned into useful action, nothing was wasted or lost. And now he was pursuing this higher aim by teaching and guiding future generations of leaders.

Prison, for him, made sense, as it did not for us, and certainly not for me. I found life in detention to be without purpose, the injustice unbearably unfair. But for my uncle, putting prison "to use" was the secret of his survival, of his calm. In analyzing and commenting succinctly the historical and political events from 1938 to the present, he demonstrated faith in the future, while his tolerance, open-mindedness, and humor glowed throughout.

He exuded moral strength and contentment: "I regret nothing," he said.

A surprising conclusion. Even more shocking in fact, was his comment: "The years I spent in prison were my happiest years."

"How can you say that?" I exclaimed, revolted at the thought. "Now, when you are surrounded by a loving and devoted wife, two wonderful sons."

"That's because in prison I was closest to Christ."

"I can understand that," said Tudor, when I shared with him my shocked puzzlement.

"You can?"

"It's an implosion. Like an outburst, but instead of being directed to the outside, it's directed inwardly. Worlds open up inside, yielding their richness."

I thought that perhaps too many years of isolation from the rest of humanity had affected the Romanians. When I was back in Paris, I shared my reaction with our French friend Simone, the physicist, when she cut in: "Yes, I can understand that." She, too? Simone reminded me of the atrocious pain her ailing eye had been causing her. One day it was absolutely excruciating, nearly unbearable, when suddenly a warm, radiant presence enveloped her in intense love, a love as she had never felt before. She remembers that moment as one of the happiest in her life.

Discovering a Soul Mate

Mihaela, accompanied by her young sons, Ion, Paul, and Mihai, brought sandwiches into my aunt and uncle's apartment. Shortly afterward, Emanuel, just back from a trip to Rome, raced wordlessly through the living room to change clothes in the bathroom so he could be all freshened up to see the relative he had last seen when he was two years old. I warmly embraced this cousin even though, as a mature eight-year-old, I had been so offended when I was exiled with him to the tots' table.

I sensed right away what I was to discover at leisure later, that Emanuel is a soul mate. We have the same sense of the world, the same passion for the country we love, the same burning need to contribute to its well-being.

We all talked, joked, ate, reminisced, laughed, reveled in family stories, sharing recollections about grandparents and uncles as I had never been able to do elsewhere. I did not have to explain anything about any family members, they all knew to whom I was referring!

Mihaela and Emanuel lived in a run-down new development, just like my aunt and uncle. Their lives had been battered, yet they radiated in their confined space the warmest, laughingest atmosphere I have seen in my extended family. Only my gentle, devoted Aunt Helga came across somewhat subdued, as if struggling after having been crushed. She seemed tense, concerned about awaiting tasks, intent on taking care of the needs of others—totally sharing my father's personality.

The next day Emanuel took me to the opening of the Congress of the Civic Alliance,[105] the beginning of the democratization process, where delegates of a variety of parties, including those representing the Hungarian and the Gypsy minorities, succeeded one another presenting their platform in an impressively constructive and orderly atmosphere. From there Emanuel introduced the four of us to the famous Village Museum, a collection of countryside dwellings that had been transported, before World War II and the Soviet occupation, from all over the country and were exhibited now in the city in a lush, pastoral setting near poetic Lake Herăstrău. Impressive folk art displayed on an intimate scale preserved a way of life that has lasted for centuries. Our daughters were enchanted.

Emanuel returned to his duties and dropped us off at Caritas where Mihaela and their son Paul awaited us: in the impressively clean, newly refurbished, hospitable and efficient kitchen, amidst the nonstop coming and going, stacking, repairing, plastering, we were served a simple but hearty vegetarian lunch consisting of *ciorbă*[106] and spaghetti with cheese. Before leaving, we were shown the 60-yard-long freshly opened warehouse and the priests' headquarters, cheerfully renovated. The country was slowly starting to pick up.

Bonding between Generations at Tudor's

"Bulevardul Dacia nr.39." Imprinted in the deepest fold of my awareness, this is the address of the Dumitraşcu family, the address where Tudor and Anca had grown up. Now, it had the supernatural quality of a dream about to materialize. I approached it with all the

---

[105]Founded on November 6, 1990 immediately after the fall of Ceauşescu and the ruling government, this Congress aimed to promote the establishment in Romania of a civil society and the rule of law, human rights and fundamental freedoms, democratic values and institutions, awareness, respect, and dissemination of truth in public life, among other similar aims.

[106]A vegetable soup with sour cabbage juice.

cautious deliberation meant to keep it from evaporating. From across the street, I took in the building's rounded corner, the second-floor balcony, the curve in the steps leading to the entrance door, all a gray version of the joyous place where, with exhilaration and the lilting step of impatient expectation, I would go to play with my little friends.

Welcoming us at the door with an open, friendly, straightforward, and slightly uncertain expression on her face was Reli, Tudor's wife, who seemed to fit seamlessly into our close-knit trio. I took to her immediately.

Inside, a new decor revealed Tudor's artistic imprint: icons, crosses in a variety of styles, peasant pottery, artwork. I saw there the religious inspiration of his creations, that almost had him imprisoned.

A little girl was then ushered in, Catinca, Tudor and Reli's daughter. I was stunned: I knew this child even though I had never met her! She was little Tudor and little Anca all rolled in one. The similarity was uncanny. I felt an instant bond with her. She might have had similar feelings, for when she shyly retired a few minutes later, I followed her to her room and she seemed totally comfortable showing me all her toys and talking, talking, talking. "Most unusual," declared Reli of her bashful daughter.

Meanwhile, Tudor had opened an album with his childhood photos to show our daughters, and they exclaimed delightedly as they went through my most precious memories: Tudor, Anca, and I at their home and at mine on Strada Paris; Anca's and my angel dance in front of the Christmas tree, a vision that had followed me through prison and exile and which I recreated with my sister at our school show in New York. Now Adriana and Domnica could see with their own eyes what for endless years I could only conjure in my mind.

At 4:30 p.m. we parted, I more reluctantly than at the previous encounter when the conversation had been more awkward. We aimed to meet again before our departure. Mircea took Adriana and Domnica with him to town and I headed to Aunt Helga and Uncle Horia's home, on my way checking out the subway recently constructed under Ceauşescu: clean, efficient, a bit old-fashioned, the names of the stations sometimes difficult to make out, but altogether a very practical system.

Last Visits at Aunt Helga and Uncle Horia's

I found my aunt and uncle alone at home and rejoiced in having more time with them, especially with Aunt Helga, so different from her self-assured and fulfilled husband and somewhat overshadowed by the male contingent of her family. Gentle, devoted, absorbed by details, she worried about all she had to take care of, again so reminiscent of her oldest brother.

After Aunt Clementina arrived together with Mihaela and Emanuel, Aunt Helga took me aside in an adjoining room and quickly, pressingly as if to take full advantage of the limited time we had together, shared some outstanding events of the past forty years of our forced separation. She unburdened what weighed most on her heart: her deep appreciation of her parents who had sustained her and her children throughout the years of her husband's incarceration and beyond; her father's acceptance of the loss of everything he had worked for and accomplished, always forging ahead and finding new solutions, an example that inspired her throughout her life. Most poignant seemed to have been her husband's court trial after he was briefly released from prison, a trial to which my grandfather had accompanied her. When her husband was convicted again to years of prison, a devastating blow, she wondered how she could face her mother and reveal the outcome. Her father consoled her as gently as he could, "Don't worry, we will find a way."

During the last years of Uncle Horia's imprisonment, Aunt Helga did not even know whether he was alive until one day, when stepping off the bus, she noticed a ragged man, staggering and leaning against a wall. "May I help you?" she offered. The man opened up to her: "I have just been released from prison," he explained and went on: "I would have committed suicide, were it not for an extraordinary, saintly fellow prisoner who brought hope back into my life, who gave me courage and strength to go on." He would never forget the man's name: Horia Cosmovici. This is how my aunt learned that her husband was alive.

Mircea and I returned one more time to my aunt and uncle's home just before our departure. With Mircea and Uncle Horia absorbed in conversation, Aunt Helga led me to the kitchen. There, the two of us became enveloped in a shroud of kinship that suddenly brought out the young woman in my 72-year-old aunt. With girlish fun and glee, we exchanged impressions and chatted and commented and joked and laughed, and laughed, and laughed.

"What are you laughing about?" came the voice from the other room. "Why don't you come sit with us?"

We dutifully (and I reluctantly) complied, and that was the end of the magical interlude. But those precious moments sank deep into my soul and I parted with my aunt and uncle feeling I had known them forever. And in them, I also found my beloved grandfather. And more.

Face-to-Face with Our Childhood Homes

With trepidation and deep emotion, Mircea and I each approached the street that would open into the world of our childhood homes. How would that world appear to us now? Would we recognize it after all the years since we last glimpsed it? At nr. 6 Strada Stupinei, now renamed Chirițescu, stood the courtyard where 14-year old Mircea had driven the family car, with an impishness that had made us laugh in recognition, years earlier, when we saw him projected in an 8mm home movie. The house was now rented by the government to foreign diplomats.[107] A German living there happened to be outside. He kindly opened the gate and led my husband in to give him a sense of the present habitation.

An intense emotion was to happen a few years later, in 2008. After nine years of filling forms, filing requests, trials, rejections, and appeals, Mircea finally obtained the return of his family home, and the keys to the house were placed in his hand. To his amazement, as he started inspecting the interior of his family's apartment, he discovered on a wall in the dining room, intact, the sketch of Dr. Nimbus (a not-very-bright comic strip character) he had drawn in 1940 as a thirteen-year old, on the plaster covering a crack from that year's earthquake!

A representative of the US Embassy in Bucharest, Bob Coleman, led us to my own neighborhood, which happened to be where he himself resided now. With Adriana and Domnica on either side of me and my arms around their shoulders, we slowly followed Bob. He led us along Bulevardul Aviatorilor and its familiar, wide, shaded sidewalks, into Piața Victoriei, unrecognizable behind its new and alien structures. Then suddenly, at a sharp angle to the left we entered Strada Paris, my street. I stared at the name. The girls were very attentive and sensitive to my reactions, but Mircea pulled a handkerchief out of his pocket and waved it in front of me, a humorous reminder that, in a lachrymal emergency, I always appeal to him for a handkerchief.

I looked at the number of one of the houses: 10. Ours was 37. A little ahead we approached the vicinity of the small square that had displayed a statue of the she-wolf that had nursed Romulus and Remus,[108] the legendary founders of the city of Rome. She was no longer there; she

[107]The Communist government had forcefully confiscated it, without compensation, in 1951, at a time of general nationalization in the country, ejecting his widowed mother and relocating her to a room on the outskirts of Bucharest, on Str. Cireşului.

[108]A gift from the City of Rome to commemorate the second-century conquest of Dacia by Roman Emperor Trajan, that gave birth to the Romanian people.

had been moved to another part of the city.[109] In her stead rose a globe of the world. It dawned on me that our house had to be close by.

With some effort, I made myself ask Bob: "How much farther to number 37?"

"It's right here!" he replied, pointing across the street, behind the abundant foliage.

I could not face it. I turned my back to it, put my head on Domnica's shoulder and cried. How much time had passed since the moment I last lived there, with my parents and my little sister, in that house I thought I would never see again. And now I was there, with my husband and our two young daughters!

Then just as suddenly, I felt I had to see it. I turned around and crossed the street. The house looked darker, narrower, and taller than I expected. I reminisced for the girls and Mircea: "There's the balcony where I decided to become an astronomer to find out what the moon knew but would not tell . . . the bedroom window where my mother had us pray for our father's return from detention . . . the flower bed where I buried my goldfish. The rose bushes are gone, but the cherry tree is still here and has cherries!! The linden tree is so tall, but no aroma. The crack in that wall is new, and so is the garbage and dirt in the yard."

The once gleaming white stairs leading to the entrance door were gray and decaying. Now inhabited by the ambassadress from Indonesia, our house was in much better shape than most, but still part of the present-day malaise. I finally gathered the courage to climb up the steps and ring the doorbell. There was no answer.

Adriana said she would love to nurse the house back to health. But it is now definitely part of another era. "My" house rests inside me, luminous in my heart and in the vivid memories it nurtures, some of which I have now been able to share with my young family.

Time to move on.

---

[109] Perhaps Piața Romană.

Connecting with the Revolution, in University Square

With only three days left before our departure, we had to split into two parties: Mircea took the girls to his father's tomb at Bellu Cemetery, where our family members are buried, while I headed for my own "cemetery": Piaţa Universităţii (University Square). There, in the spring of 1990, after the fall of Ceauşescu, students, joined by thousands of citizens of all ages, had demonstrated day and night in support of free elections and against the "Neo-Communist" members of Ceauşescu's government who were attempting to grab power, resonating with the weeks of agitation and strikes in the entire country. From the echoes that reached us across the Atlantic, I knew these had been intense days of discussion, hope, planning, speeches, and solidarity.

As I tried to resurrect in my mind the effervescence of the event, soaked in hope, I scanned the buildings plastered with signs, some in Chinese characters obviously inspired by the events in Tian An Men Square. The signs called for democracy and expressed gratitude for all those who had sacrificed their lives in the December 1989 revolution, in an effort to thrust off the remnants of dictatorship after Ceauşescu's execution. I deciphered the hand-written words of the traditional song "*Deşteaptă-te Române*," which called for the awakening of Romanians. It is now Romania's national anthem (my translation):

> *Wake up, Romanian, from the sleep of death*
> *Into which barbaric tyrants plunged you.*
> *Now or nevermore carve your own destiny"*

I strived to visualize the spot where students had delimited a "zone free of Neo-Communism." In peaceful demonstrations that had lasted for weeks, they had called for the erection of a Statue of Liberty in front of the nearby National Theater and declared solidarity with the Chinese students of Tian An Men. On June 13, 1990, these protesters were brutally, sometimes lethally, disbanded by club-wielding miners who had been called in all the way from the Carpathian Mountains by the newly and irregularly elected "neo-Communist" president, Ion Iliescu.[110, 111] I recalled Mihaela's description of the terror spread by the miners, who chased anyone and everyone they encountered in the streets of Bucharest, and of seeking refuge in the entrance of any open building. I deposited a bouquet of flowers at the monument dedicated to the memory of those who had died in December 1989, as well as at the cross dedicated to the *golani*,[112] the so-called rascals who had pressed for democracy and fell in June 1990.

I watched an old woman remove dried leaves and petals and sweep the place clean with a broom fashioned from the dry branches of a tree. Then I left.

Before our final departure, we visited one last Bucharest landmark that anchors our family to the city, not far from where Uncle Valter and cousin Rucky lived on Vasile Lascăr Street. The street opens onto a large, busy square with shops and bus and tram stations. There, on an island in its midst, stands the statue of my mother's great-grandfather, Constantin A. (C. A.) Rosetti (1816–1885). A revolutionary patriot striving for the independence and unity of the Romanian people in the wake of the 1848 revolutions in Europe, Rosetti is one of the founders of modern Romania. He fought for the liberation of the serfs and for the

---

[110]"The Bush administration called home the US ambassador to Romania Thursday to protest the intimidation of opposition candidates and other irregularities that have marred the campaign for the country's first multi-party election in more than 40 years." (*Los Angeles Times*, May 11, 1990).

[111]Romania's former President Ion Iliescu has now been charged with crimes against humanity for his role in the aftermath of the violent revolt that toppled the communist regime in 1989 (*BBC World News*, April 8, 2019. See https://www.bbc.com/world-Europe-47858664).

[112]"Golani" means "rascals," a derogatory epithet affixed by Iliescu to the demonstrators and worn as a badge of honor by all those who joined in.

Adriana and Domnica with me at the foot of the C.A. Rosetti statue in Bucharest.

distribution of land to the peasants. He succeeded in the first endeavor during his lifetime, in 1856, shortly before slaves were freed in the United States. His second endeavor had to wait for the beginning of the twentieth century. His detractors sneeringly dubbed him "the American" due to his democratic ideas. I took my daughters to his statue and presented them to him: "Great-great-grandfather, it is with immense joy and pride that I bring to you now your American descendants. (In time, he would have an American descendant named after him, my daughter Domnica's son and my grandson, Adrian Constantin.)

Return to the USA, July 9, 1991

On the eve of our departure, Tudor stopped by to listen to my presentation, taped at the ARA conference. Now, there was no more awkwardness, only warmth when we hugged to say good-bye. That was the last time I was to see him.[113]

---

[113]Two years later, Domnica called me from Bucharest after visiting the Dumitraşcu family and gently broke the news that Tudor had suddenly died of a heart attack. The mildness of my reaction surprised her. "My world died when we escaped from Romania and we became almost totally cut off from it," I explained. "It was miraculously resurrected for a little while and I absorbed all the joy of reconnecting with it. But now it is back to normal: dead."

The next day, all aboard on a British Aircraft Corporation BAC-11, TAROM flight 381, we sat in a warm embrace two and two behind each other, cheerful smiles on our faces, gleams in our eyes: "We seem so happy yet we have just seen such horror."

What we saw was shocking, indeed distressing: the dilapidation of the city, the derailed economy, the dearth of the necessities of life, the population's lack of hope.

Whence the glorious feeling?

From the human reconnections: Tudor, who intrigued and captivated the girls just as he did their mother 43 years earlier; Emanuel and Mihaela, whose altruism filled their life and ours with zest; Aunt Helga and Uncle Horia, whose boundless caring and acceptance enveloped us in the magic of roots; Uncle Valter, Rucky, Ileana, and Aunt Clementina, who filled our horizon with close-knit kinship; Cuca who treated us to a treasured glimpse into her exquisite art; Mircea's lifelong friends, who embraced us with their liveliness and hospitality; Simona, who allowed us to invade her quarters with a cheerful and genuine welcome. From the friendliness of the local population in general, including strangers who, even if some appeared grouchy or reclusive, ended up, like hard candy with a soft filling, spreading their basic good will. From the deeply nourishing human warmth of these encounters.

"Are you sad to leave?" inquired Adriana.

Not really. We absorbed more than I had ever dared hope. Time now to settle down and assimilate the wealth of spirituality, wisdom, selflessness, kindness, and friendship that had been poured on us. "They have so little yet give so much," observed a friend who had preceded us in Romania. A perfect summing up.

But Mircea fumed: "I am even angrier at them now for the destruction they have wrought on the country."

"Why now? We have known it all along."

"Yes, intellectually. But now I have seen it physically and I cannot forgive them for this senseless devastation."

Ingrid, Domnica, Mircea, and Adriana at the time of our return trip.

As feelings and sensations settled and sorted out over the following days and weeks, Adriana wondered: "Are you happy you went?" while shuddering herself at the thought she might have missed the experience. Now, she explained, she would no longer take things for granted. She can understand pain and how it affects people. She understands this other way of life and the hope the future holds.

Domnica joined in: "Now we understand where our parents come from. Now I understand who I am."

For Mircea and me, it was unthinkable not to go. I had to go as I had to live once I was born. The return glued the pieces together. It tethered me to myself; it snapped together the past and the present, the child and the adult; it injected life into my amputated and reattached emotional limbs; it flooded with light the darkness in my being: I am whole again. I now feel free to grow deep, solid roots into the US soil. No longer a foreigner, no longer a refugee, no longer an immigrant.

EPILOGUE: ROOTS AGAIN

Roots can be multiple and stretch around the world. And roots wind in and out among the loves and friendships you yourself have created.

—Dedication on the journal my friends
Ann, Silvia, and Susan gifted me to
record our return trip to Romania.

Intense rejoicing, celebrations and fireworks marked two history-changing events for Romania that followed shortly after the upheavals of 1989.

In 2004, Romania was granted a much-yearned-for membership in NATO, entering thus the secure fortress that might protect the country from future invasions.

In 2007, Romania joined the European Union, affording it interaction with the European countries for which it has the greatest affinity and from which it was totally cut off over the more than four decades of sequestration in the Soviet sphere of influence.

The changes in the country after that time became obvious in our subsequent trips to Romania. Despite the painful demands on the population required to bring it to West European levels, the scarred faces of the cities were being rejuvenated, painted in bright colors; Western-style groceries and restaurants opened everywhere; the latest electronic technology became available. Taking advantage of the new ease of movement and newly paved roads paid for with European funds, we went exploring: the unique medieval painted churches of Bucovina, which I discovered then for the first time with Domnica and her Romanian friend, pianist Horia Mihail, who drove us there; the imposing Făgăraş Mountains that harbored the resistance to the Soviet occupation; the university town of Braşov, where my cousin Mihaela (Uncle Eugen's daughter) guided us through the ski areas, suggesting a parallel between Braşov and Boulder, Colorado (possible sister cities?).

Our 2012 trip, centered on Cluj, stands out by the poetry of the Maramureş hillsides and the border town of Sighet, site of the Memorial of the Victims of Communism and of the Resistance, where truth is

In Cluj in 2012: Mircea (right, center) with my cousins Emanuel and Mihaela (on Mircea's left), and their son Andrei (next to Mircea) and (left, center) Andrei's wife Aliodora, with their children Tereza and Iuliu.

at last being revealed. There, on a previous trip with friends, Domnica had left in a state of shock after unexpectedly sighting, in the cell devoted to women prisoners, a photograph of my mother, and then one of me.

In Cluj, I bonded with Iuliu, the little grandson of my cousin Emanuel, whom I love to call my grandnephew. He looked at me one evening as I was tenderly putting him to bed and said: "You look like Grandma," "And," I replied: "you look like my father."

Skype and telephone conversations now fill the gaping void that had stretched over so long an absence and nourish my soul, releasing it from the pain of the rending separation.

In 1990, after the opening of the Romanian borders, we founded the Romanian American Freedom Alliance, a charitable organization in the United States that provides a constant stream of assistance to orphaned or abandoned children and families in need in Romania. Thus, a rewarding ongoing bridge between the two countries has been established.

New Shoots

Freed from the grip of my trauma, I could now let sink in the roots that, over the decades, had timidly started inching their way on this continent, sensitized to the friendships that bind me to this land, to the startling beauty of the country with which I was slowly falling in love and to healing aspects of life in the United States, as conjured by the following remembrances.

* * *

Exhilarated by the Pulse of a Metropolis

New York, the international crossroads where we settled after our arrival in the United States: the stimulation of a metropolis, of glistening glass canyons that echo its vivifying frenzy; of shows, museums, parks; of avenues and department stores metamorphosing into a fairyland at Christmastime—all of the above inspired in me an enthusiastic love that now mirrors my passion for Romania. Time, stretching the distance to my adolescence, allows me now to point out New York to my daughters as the place "where I grew up," engendering a sense of contentedness with my surroundings there that I had not felt since leaving Romania.

Nestled in the Boulder Foothills

One afternoon I rode my bike home from work, along tree-lined 12th Street on "the hill." In the distance, the sharp silhouette of the Flatirons appeared behind the red-tiled roofs. Suddenly, the aroma of a linden tree filled my lungs and I felt focused on the present moment as I never do, its beauty, its perfume no longer jarred by my childhood recollection of the linden tree by our house in Bucharest. Is there at last a bridge over the chasm that tore asunder my childhood?

My Childhood Reshaped by My Younger Daughter's Schooling

From my diary: "I sense that my younger daughter Adriana will pull me out of prison. There is this double, parallel life, in which I relive my childhood with her, but I also live her childhood. It's as if my childhood were grafted onto hers and it is "replayed" with a different script. I know the course of the past events, but their flavor, their meaning, is changed. With Adriana, I will be 8 years old again, but in the vibrant, fulfilling setting of the Flatirons School in Boulder. I have been in prison, secluded, stunted and deeply wounded. My wings have been severed but they will grow again and I will take off with my younger daughter. Suddenly, there is so much more to my 9th year, because through Adriana I discover laughter, joy, fancy English words like "gullible" and "biblical admonitions"; I learn to make Indian teepees and xylophones from slabs of Colorado stone, I admire such unexpected, and, for my background, far-out idols like Michael Jackson and Martin Luther King. Mainly I can absorb like a sponge, with an 8-years-old enthusiasm and sparkle, all the wonders of knowledge and nature, of people, of life, so absent in our detention and so lavishly bestowed here."

Strolling in Colorado's Past

Shaded by tender aspen leaves on a Sunday morning, my husband and I strolled on the quiet, sunlit streets of the old mining town of Georgetown, soothed by the murmur of two connecting creeks that flow gently behind cheerful little houses built to the size of a human, with bridges running back and forth between the yards. Slow-paced, joyful, regenerating, they brought up a faraway reminiscence of the countryside of our childhood.

The Joy of Voting

In November I experienced, at the Boulder voting polls, the joy of seeing again volunteers Mickey and Carol, of having Margot call to make sure we vote. I absorb the warmth of this community and its dedication to our democracy. Do I finally belong? Is my journey reaching port at last?

Returning Home One Evening

One night, as Mircea and I drove back from a full day in Denver, the sky was magically clear, speckled with little movie-set clouds. The deep blue silhouette of the mountains sparkled here and there with the evening lights. As the first waves of the Rockies pressed against each other and we approached Boulder, I thought: This is home. No other place after Romania had felt like this. This feels like home again, at last.

* * *

The definitive anchoring, though, came when I worked toward a Colorado teaching license for the secondary level to achieve a closer relationship with my students after several years of research at Boulder's National Oceanic and Atmospheric Administration Laboratory and teaching at the Colorado School of Mines and at Metropolitan State College.

Substitute teaching throughout the Boulder Valley School District, I came upon an institution that stole my heart: Summit Charter Middle School in Boulder. Recently founded by a group of parents with the aim of challenging students and nestled in temporary portables in another school's backyard, limited in its amenities, this special school was a haven for the most "awake," interested, lively yet respectful students I had encountered. The ten minutes the Spanish teacher spent explaining to me what I was expected to do in her class signaled what I was soon to discover on my own as part of its faculty: the total dedication of the teachers to their students. With open arms, my colleagues welcomed me, and I could share in the galvanizing atmosphere inspired by two successive principals and fed by the input of the parents who quite readily invested long hours and multifaceted talents to make Summit possible. Everyone's openness and willingness to listen, to respond to our concerns, combined with a climate of warm collegiality, allowed me to flourish both as a teacher and as a human being. The twelve and a half years I taught at Summit are among the happiest in my life.

Even more important, every year I was invited into the World Geography classes to share my experience with the Soviet occupation and its ramifications. This experience allowed me to impart to new generations a knowledge that had so heavily weighed on me, and in so doing to slowly heal. Healing, I was freed to live in the present, to become a part of the community where I live, to grow roots here, to become fully integrated in Summit's vibrant and nurturing environment and, by extension, in Colorado.

New Roots

Having moved from culture to culture for most of my formative years, I thought I would forever hear "Where are you from?"—a question I was at a loss to answer.

Now I know. I am from a string of places: The center of my existence has slipped away from Romania, squeezed through Yugoslavia, pulled enriched identity in Paris and in New York, finally sinking roots in Boulder, Colorado, with multiple tentacles stretching everywhere we have friends and newfound family. My home, my roots, are now solidly entrenched here in the land where we rebuilt our lives, where an intense and relentless pursuit of fairness and democracy exist, free to devote ourselves to the endeavors we choose, free to be who we are, to merge into a blessed oneness that allows me to be fully American without erasing my Romanian identity, admitted into the brilliance of the quilt we all engender. My home, my roots are now in the land that is so close to our daughters' hearts, the land of their birth and of our rebirth, the United States of America.

Gate in Maramureş region, Romania, with a view of the road that leads to the monastery.

APPENDIX A
THE ECONOMU FAMILY

On August 27, 2001, when Romanian television aired my interview about our escape from Yugoslavia 51 years after the event, a member of the Economu family, Zelma Sfetescu, Mrs. Economu's niece, happened to see it. She contacted the producer, Lucia Hossu Longin, eager to know more.

Two weeks later, I spoke at length with Zelma. The following information is from my telephone conversation with her.

Sandu and Liliana's parents were Elena (born Sfetescu) and Narcis Economu. Elena Sfetescu was from Bucharest and had three brothers, Mircea, Nicu, and Eugen, who was Zelma's father. Zelma (born in 1935) and her cousins, Sandu (born in 1931) and Liliana (born in 1933), would spend summers at the Black Sea resort town of Eforie Sud. They had great fun putting on plays for the neighbors, directed by Aunt Elena, who was very gifted and beloved by the children.

Elena Economu's German-born mother, Zelma Lipman, died without ever learning about the fate of her daughter and her grandchildren.

Narcis Economu had no relatives except for a niece, Viorica, who was a granddaughter of the famous Romanian painter Ştefan Luchian. Narcis had been involved in politics and was under surveillance. One day the secret police came to his house when he was out. As he was returning home, Sandu and Liliana saw him coming and signaled to him from the window not to come in. Narcis then fled to the Banat province where he worked as a forestry engineer in Bârzava. His wife and children followed him there. Members of his family have no idea when nor how they escaped. (Subsequently I tried to find among our refugee friends who were still alive someone who could provide this information, but I could not).

After the Economu's escape, Zelma's father (Mrs. Economu's brother) was fired and was no longer allowed to be employed because his sister had escaped. His house was taken away and his family all moved into a single room. Twenty years later they heard from Radio Madrid that the Economu couple and their children had been killed in Romania (with no mention of Yugoslavia).

APPENDIX B
MY MATERNAL GRANDPARENTS

Mihai Gavrilescu

(7 November 1873 in Bivolari, Iaşi County–
29 February 1944 in Bucharest)

By the time he had reached the age of eleven, my maternal grandfather, **Mihai Gavrilescu**, an only child, lost his father, Alexandru Gavrilescu (in 1875, when Mihai was only three), his mother, Maria Chiper (four years later) and, in 1883 when he was eleven, his aunt Aneta Gavrilescu, who had taken him in. To sign up the orphaned child in Romania's naval school, those in charge of him lied about his age and said he was twelve, the minimum age required for acceptance. My grandfather thus grew up on the naval training vessel *Bricul Mircea*. He must have been treated very well because all his life he expressed the deepest affection for the Navy, in which he eventually reached the rank of vice-admiral, earning numerous distinctions. For example, in 1993, almost fifty years after his death, a corvette (a small warship) in the Romanian Navy was renamed *Vice-Admiral Mihai Gavrilescu* in his honor.

In his thirties, Mihai Gavrilescu took a young bride, Alina Rosetti, fifteen years his junior. Alina unfortunately did not survive a tuberculosis epidemic and died a few years later, in May 1916, at the age of

28, shortly before Romania was to enter World War I, leaving her husband with two young daughters: my mother Ariane, age five and a half, and her sister Lydia, age four. Being away on ships much of the time, Mihai enrolled his daughters in the Notre Dame de Sion boarding school in Galaţi. He kept a close watch on his daughters' care and education, providing the French nuns with port wine to be given regularly to his daughters as protection against tuberculosis (the belief of the times), and insisting his daughters obtain baccalaureate degrees, even though the nuns did not educate their students to that level. He wanted to make sure (in the 1920s!) that his daughters were well prepared for life and capable to fend on their own. They both went on to earn master's degrees, my mother in mathematics, my aunt in French and Italian languages and in Romanian literature. He also took his daughters with him on some of his assignments: the trip to Italy when she was not yet twelve remained one of my mother's most indelible memories—one that she would recall with emotion and delight into her old age. Perhaps less enjoyable but still memorable was his insistence that his daughters listen to classical music in total darkness, the better to absorb it. My grandfather loved music and named his first daughter Ariane, after the title of Jules Massenet's opera, which he had seen in Paris before her birth.

Despite his repeated losses, my grandfather was positive and optimistic, and he often stated that he was afraid of nothing. This is a source of great strength for me and, I hope, for future generations of descendants. His compassion is an example and a source of inspiration as well: his comment regarding a man condemned for some misdeed was: "The poor man. Who knows what the circumstances of his life are?"

Alina Rosetti

(24 January 1888–30 May 1916 in Bucharest)

Alina Rosetti was the granddaughter of one of the founding fathers of modern Romania, C. A. Rosetti. When she was six years old, her 27-year-old mother, Elisa Iatropol, passed away, and her father, Vintilă Rosetti, married the governess, who lived up to some of the worst reputations for stepmothers: she seized every opportunity to hurt her stepdaughter and even her two young step-granddaughters.

Despite the pain in her childhood, Alina grew up to be a cheerful and vivacious young woman. After marriage to Mihai Gavrilescu in her early twenties, she gave birth to two daughters, Ariane (September 1910) and Lydia (January 1912), only seventeen months apart. It is believed that this may have weakened her immune system; she subsequently came down with tuberculosis. Facing now the prospect that her daughters could experience the trauma of her own childhood, a prospect that (as I know from personal experience) can be much, much worse than living that trauma oneself, she asked her husband to promise he would not remarry. My grandfather kept that promise. He also kept, until the end of his life, the ticket for the excursion where he had met his future bride.

My mother's bedtime stories were often visited by recollections of her own mother, passing on to me a feeling of gentleness and tenderness.

Alina's name, and thus her memory, has now been kept for at least four successive generations beyond hers:

Ariane Alina, her daughter
Ingrid Alina, her granddaughter
Alina Domnica, her great-granddaughter
Alina Linda, her great-great-granddaughter . . .

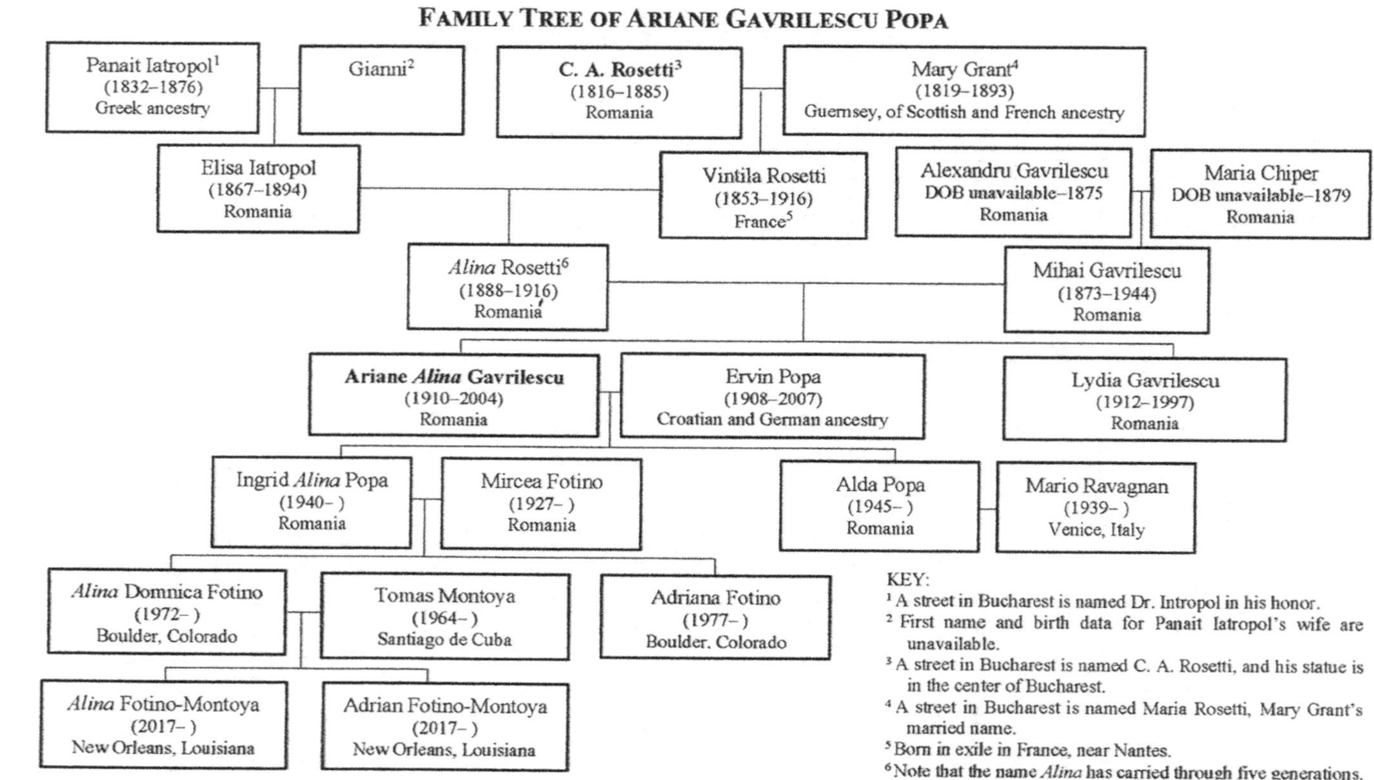
FAMILY TREE OF ARIANE GAVRILESCU POPA
Panait Iatropol[1]
(1832–1876)
Greek ancestry
Gianni[2]
C. A. Rosetti[3]
(1816–1885)
Romania
Mary Grant[4]
(1819–1893)
Guernsey, of Scottish and French ancestry
Elisa Iatropol
(1867–1894)
Romania
Vintila Rosetti
(1853–1916)
France[5]
Alexandru Gavrilescu
DOB unavailable–1875
Romania
Maria Chiper
DOB unavailable–1879
Romania
Alina Rosetti[6]
(1888–1916)
Romania
Mihai Gavrilescu
(1873–1944)
Romania
Ariane Alina Gavrilescu
(1910–2004)
Romania
Ervin Popa
(1908–2007)
Croatian and German ancestry
Lydia Gavrilescu
(1912–1997)
Romania
Ingrid Alina Popa
(1940–)
Romania
Mircea Fotino
(1927–)
Romania
Alda Popa
(1945–)
Romania
Mario Ravagnan
(1939–)
Venice, Italy
Alina Domnica Fotino
(1972–)
Boulder, Colorado
Tomas Montoya
(1964–)
Santiago de Cuba
Adriana Fotino
(1977–)
Boulder, Colorado
Alina Fotino-Montoya
(2017–)
New Orleans, Louisiana
Adrian Fotino-Montoya
(2017–)
New Orleans, Louisiana
KEY:
1 A street in Bucharest is named Dr. Intropol in his honor.
2 First name and birth data for Panait Iatropol's wife are unavailable.
3 A street in Bucharest is named C. A. Rosetti, and his statue is in the center of Bucharest.
4 A street in Bucharest is named Maria Rosetti, Mary Grant's married name.
5 Born in exile in France, near Nantes.
6 Note that the name Alina has carried through five generations.

APPENDIX C
MY AUNT LYDIA'S INCARCERATION DOCUMENTS

Lydia Gavrilescu, probably age 47.

My Aunt Lydia Gavrilescu harbored a Greek Catholic priest at a time when such priests were persecuted. This was the reason for her incarceration, stated as *activitate contra-revoluționară* (counter-revolutionary activity). The following are copies of her criminal matriculation file.

S.F. Pol. POLITIC V.27 ...

PENITENCIARUL Jilava | Pol. | O Nr. MATRICOL 1830.

Anul 1951 luna Iulie ziua 17

FIŞA MATRICOLĂ PENALĂ

2) Lista 28/62

1. NUMELE Gavrilescu Pronumele Lidia

Porecla Elena

2. Născut în anul 1912 luna Ianuarie ziua 18 în Comuna Galați

Raionul Regiunea Galați

3. Fica lui Mihail + şi al Olivia +

4. Domiciliat în Comuna Bucur. Str. Spătarului Nr. 37

Raionul 1 Mai Regiunea București

5. Ocupaţiunea, în prezent Prof. infirmieră în trecut idem

6. Averea deţinutei în prezent f. avere

în trecut idem

7. Ocupaţia soţului în prezent necăsăt. în trecut —

8. Averea soţ — în prezent —

în trecut —

9. Ocupaţia părinţilor în prezent decedat.

în trecut amiral.

10. Averea părinţilor, în prezent decedați

în trecut f. avere

11. Originea socială burgheză

12. Cetăţenia română studii licent. in litere

13. Starea civilă necăsăt. numele soţ — copii băeţi — fete —

14. Serviciul militar : ctg. — gradul — unitatea căreia aparţine —

15. Apartenenţa politică a deţinutei în prezent f. m. p.

în trecut apolitică

16. Starea sănătăţii (ce defecte fizice şi psihice are)

SEMNALMENTE: talia 1.57 m. fruntea mijl. nasul mijl. gura mijl. bărbia mijl.

faţa ovală ochii căpr. părul cast. sprâncenele cast. barba —

urechea mijl. mustaţa — semne particulare nu are

SITUAŢIA JURIDICĂ :

a) ANTECEDENTELE PENALE

Dacă este infractor din obicei

b) PREVENIT, depus de Parch. Mil. Buc. la 29 X 951 cu mandatul de arestare Nr. 12969 /1951 pentru fapt activitate contrarevoluționară, J. 25703/951

Descrierea pe scurt a faptului

Prin ordonanţa definitivă Nr. — /195 — emisă de — rămas sub stare de arest până la terminarea judecăţii.

c) INTERNAT, de către D. G. S. S. cu ordinul Nr. 413.616/951

Se mai menţine ca $\frac{\text{prevenit}}{\text{internat}}$ cu $\frac{\text{mandat}}{\text{ordin}}$ N-rele

Eşiri provizorii

Reprimiri din eşiri provizorii

Pedepse disciplinare

Purtarea Cum a muncit

Eşiri definitive

d) CONDAMNAT ____ imatricolat în ziua de ____ primit dela ____

Numărul mandatului şi instanţa care l-a emis	Numărul hotărârei judecătoreşti şi instanţa care a pronunţat-o	Fapta comisă, articolul, codul sau legea în care se încadrează	Durata şi felul pedepsei	Comutări, reduceri, graţieri, adăugiri, computări, contopiri	Data începerii pedepsei Anul	Luna	Ziua	Data expirări pedepsei Anul	Luna	Ziua
897/52 T. Mil. Buc	396/52 T. Mil. Buc	Uneltire contra ord. soc	4 ani cor. 80 zile	Conf. decret 544/954 anulează	1951	I	24	1955	I	23
					1951	I	24	1955	IV	

Descrierea pe scurt a faptului: Agăzduit pe preotul Lelutiu Greco-catolic

Descrierea pe scurt a faptului:

Descrierea pe scurt a faptului:

Descrierea pe scurt a faptului:

Descrierea pe scurt a faptului:

Observaţiuni ____

Eşiri provizorii (transferări în afaceri judiciare, spitale, evadări) 10 V 1952 transf. Mislea f. 13984/952

Reprimiri din eşiri provizorii ____
Transferări definitive ____
Cum a muncit şi meseria însuşită ____
Premii, evidenţieri ____
Şcoli urmate în penitenciar ____
Pedepse disciplinare ____

Purtarea ____
Readaptat sau nu ____
Eşiri definitive 23-I-1955 Eliberată prin expirarea pedepsei
Plasat în câmpul muncii ____

Impresiunea degetului arătător stâng

Semnătura deţinut [signature]

Fişa a fost întocmită de [signature]
Verificat şi găsit în conformitate cu actele de deţinere la dosar.

DIRECTOR, [signature]

Secretar de grefă, [signature]

Father Gâldău.

APPENDIX D
THE PRIESTS

Father Leu

(March 1903–August 1983)

After their daring escape from Yugoslavia in January 1949, Father Leu and Father Gâldău reached Austria, from whence, under the aegis of the World Council of Churches, they proceeded to London. Elected bishop by a group of high Romanian prelates who were organizing resistance to the forced Communist takeover of the churches, Father Leu traveled throughout Western Europe and the Near East to accomplish his mission. He tended to the Romanian Orthodox Communities outside Romania's borders and to the needs of the influx of refugees, while also exposing the dramatic situation of the Romanian Church under the Soviet-imposed regime. In August 1952, having failed in its attempts to assassinate him, the Soviet KGB[114] kidnapped Father Leu from a train station in Austria. For the next twelve years he was to be submitted to torture and imprisonment in some of the most brutal centers of Communist "reeducation,"[115] first at Ljubljanka in the Soviet Union,

[114]KGB, Commissariat for State Security, the dreaded Soviet security apparatus.

[115]"Reeducation" is a euphemism for the breaking down of a prisoner through isolation, hunger, and torture until he or she "confessed" what the government wanted to hear, or accepted to collaborate with the secret police, either in spying on others or convincing others to join the Communist Party and cooperate with them.

then at Piteşti, Văcăreşti, Dej, Gherla, Aiud, and Jilava in Romania.[116] In 1964, after pressure from the president of the United States, Lyndon Johnson, Romania's prisons were emptied of their political prisoners, including my uncle, Horia Cosmovici, and Father Leu. The latter resumed his pastoral activity, overcoming a variety of Communist government-inspired impediments until his death in 1983. He is buried at the Cernica Monastery near Bucharest.

In a May 2006 letter to his nephew Paul Leu, jurist Maria Matei commented, echoing exactly some of my feelings as a child: "He spoke so beautifully, pouring his soul into his words, he knew so much, he was so well documented, that we could have listened to him for days on end without needing anything else."[117]

Father Gâldău

(February 27, 1903–December 11, 1991)

Father Gâldău was considered a spy by the Soviet-imposed Communist government for having helped American General Skyler distribute aid received from the United States. He was put on trial, and his belongings were confiscated. He escaped from Romania to Yugoslavia by jumping out of a train on Yugoslav territory.

For years I was spellbound by his account of his escape from the prison in Kovačica, together with Father Leu and a young man named Ionel, after he found out that he was meant to be returned to Romania in exchange for Yugoslav General Popovici. The general had opposed Tito and escaped to Romania, where he was being held prisoner.

The main feats of that incredible journey:

---

[116]Paul Leu, "Răpit de KGB şi condamnat la moarte," Ed. Euroland, Suceava, 2009.

[117]Paul Leu, "Răpit de KGB şi condamnat la moarte," Ed. Euroland, Suceava, 2009, p. 406. My translation.

- **Obtaining a copy of the key** to the prison door from Ion Ardeleanu, a prisoner employed by the prison's commandant for his exceptional mechanical skills. Ardeleanu, who was privy to the commandant's phone conversations (due to the lack of privacy inherent to the candlestick phone he used), was the one who warned Father Gâldău of the planned exchange of prisoners;
- **Climbing over the prison wall** in the early morning hours of January 7, 1949, pulled by the other two, while the neighborhood dogs started barking and the guard who came out to check on the wall missed both Father Gâldău, crouching at the foot of the wall, and the two others who had made it to the top of the wall. (The previous evening, Father Gâldău had paid the prison tailor to keep the guards drinking wine he had brought with him, bought with money obtained by selling his watch during an outing to town to bring back drinking water);
- **Riding on an open train car** that carried coal, in which they hid to escape control;
- **Arriving in a train station that was surrounded by guards** and where no one could leave without showing their identity card (everybody had to be looking for them). They watched two very self-assured men in drab clothes pass the control without showing anything, simply saying, "zdravo!"[118]; they successfully followed suit!
- **Hiding in haystacks near the border with Austria** while the dogs who chased them lost their track because it started to rain.
- **Throwing themselves repeatedly into a ditch** along a road leading to the border every time a border police car passed by (every 10 or 15 minutes).

[118] Standard Serbian salutation.

- **Being suddenly enveloped at night by a cloud** that totally concealed them from a guard at the border with Austria who was coming toward them with an electric light, alerted by the reverberating bark of a dog.
- **Navigating the treacherous path across the border**, avoiding the border control and slipping between two houses about a yard and a half apart with the help of Ionel, who had already attempted that crossing once before and had been caught;
- **Finally reaching Austria** with shouts of joy.

After his arrival in London, Father Gâldău's ties with the Anglican Church were of great assistance. These ties dated back to his assignment, several years earlier, to the Anglican Church in Bucharest, as the Soviets did not allow pastors from Great Britain to come to occupied Romania. After a stint serving Sts Constantine and Helen, the first Romanian Orthodox parish established in London under the aegis of the World Council of Churches, Father Gâldău was appointed in 1955 to St Dumitru's parish in New York, where we happily renewed our ties of appreciation, respect, and friendship. After repeated efforts, in 1963 he finally succeeded in bringing his wife, Maria, out of Romania, and in 1964 their two sons, Radu and Sandu, after a payment of $15,000 to the Romanian Communist government. Until his retirement in 1982, he actively assisted Romanian refugees, working with several religious or secular organizations, giving with boundless generosity. He spent his remaining years lovingly surrounded by his family, which now included three grandsons.

Appendix E
Churchill's Iron Curtain Speech

The following excerpts are from Winston Churchill's Sinews of Peace speech, also known as the Iron Curtain speech, at Westminster College in Fulton, Missouri, on March 5, 1946.

A shadow has fallen upon the scenes so lately lighted by the Allied victory. Nobody knows what Soviet Russia and its Communist international organization intends to do in the immediate future, or what are the limits, if any, to their expansive and proselytizing tendencies.

From Stettin in the Baltic to Trieste in the Adriatic an iron curtain has descended across the Continent. Behind that line lie all the capitals of the ancient states of Central and Eastern Europe. Warsaw, Berlin, Prague, Vienna, Budapest, Belgrade, Bucharest and Sofia, all these famous cities and the populations around them lie in what I must call the Soviet sphere, and all are subject in one form or another, not only to Soviet influence but to a very high and, in some cases, increasing measure of control from Moscow. . . .

The Communist parties, which were very small in all these Eastern States of Europe, have been raised to pre-eminence and power far beyond their numbers and are seeking everywhere to obtain totalitarian control. Police governments are prevailing in nearly every case. . . .

An attempt is being made by the Russians in Berlin to build up a quasi-Communist party in their zone of occupied Germany by showing special favors to groups of left-wing German leaders. At the end of the fighting last June, the American and British Armies withdrew westward, in accordance with an earlier agreement, to a depth at some points of 150 miles upon a front of nearly four hundred miles, in order to allow our Russian allies to occupy this vast expanse of territory which the Western Democracies had conquered.

Appendix F
Letter from French Diplomat Robert Morisset

In this letter, dated March 8,1987, Robert Morisset, the French diplomat stationed at the French Embassy in Belgrade at the time of our detention, recounts the secret and colorful meeting he had, in May 1949, with a former Yugoslav partisan, now highly placed. The Yugoslav's young daughter had tuberculosis and Monsieur Morisset had obtained for him the necessary medication from Switzerland, unavailable in Yugoslavia. When the partisan (who remained nameless) asked what he could do to express his gratitude, Monsieur Morisset mentioned refugees detained in Yugoslavia whom he would like to see released to France. Subsequently, a procedure that would allow the refugees indicated by Monsieur Morisset to leave Yugoslavia and reach France was arranged with the Yugoslav Ministry of Foreign Affairs and its French counterpart (the Quai d'Orsay).

The procedure worked reasonably well as time passed, with dramatic exceptions, such as the killing of the Economu family. Monsieur Morisset, lamenting their execution, surmises that such incidents were due to certain local authorities who were particularly slow to accept the

1949 break with Moscow, feeling nostalgia for the Cominform.[119] The Cominform allowed Stalin to control the European Communist parties. Initially located in Belgrade, it then moved to Bucharest at the time of the break of Yugoslavia's government with Moscow.

---

[119]The Communist Information Bureau established in September 1947 to exchange information among nine European Communist parties and to coordinate their activities.

C'est au début de l'année 1949 que nous parvint, à l'Ambassade, la rumeur que des ressortissants des pays communistes voisins, trompés par la propagande du Kominform qui présentait Tito comme un traître ayant vendu son pays aux Américains, tentaient par tous les moyens de gagner la Yougoslavie, croyant y trouver les Occidentaux et la liberté ; qu'en fait ils étaient soit refoulés dans leur pays d'origine soit internés dans des camps.

Il fallut attendre mai 1949 pour avoir confirmation de cette rumeur. Un soir que je travaillais tard (vers 19h30) à l'Ambassade – j'y étais pratiquement seul avec le portier français (un ancien sous-officier de la Légion étrangère dont la loyauté et la discrétion étaient à toute épreuve) – ce dernier me téléphona qu'il venait d'ouvrir la grille à un monsieur insistant qui se disait roumain, parlant bien français et demandait à voir un fonctionnaire de l'Ambassade. Je descendis donc dans le hall et vis un monsieur distingué, assez âgé qui paraissait très fatigué. Il me dit s'appeler Criban, être un ancien ministre roumain, avoir, comme nombre de ses compatriotes, fui le régime communiste, et travailler, sans doute grâce à son ancienne condition, dans une entreprise de la région de Belgrade. Comme il avait obtenu l'autorisation de venir consulter un médecin et que ses deux "accompagnateurs" étaient allés voir leur famille et lui avaient donné rendez-vous à (20) 8 heures pour repartir, il avait sauté sur l'occasion pour venir à l'ambassade où il demandait asile - Je lui expliquai les difficultés d'une telle solution, lui demandant de rentrer à son entreprise et lui promettant que nous ferions tout pour essayer de le faire partir régulièrement - Je téléphonai alors à ma femme pour lui demander d'apporter tous les médicaments de première nécessité que nous avions (aspirine, lactéol, vitamines etc) - Elle les lui remit et il nous quitta après nous avoir chaleureusement remerciés ainsi que le portier -

Restait à tenir ma promesse - J'expliquai le tout à l'ambassadeur, M. Payart, le lendemain matin - Il fut évidemment très intéressé, me dit qu'il ne pouvait s'occuper personnellement de l'affaire - ce qui était évident - mais qu'il me laissait carte blanche et en avisait Paris - C'est là que la chance se manifesta sous la forme d'un rapprochement de situations :

le long délai pour obtenir un appartement "diplomatique" à Belgrade, nous avait obligés à vivre plusieurs mois à l'hôtel Majestic, l'hôtel pour étrangers. Le temps aidant, nous avions établi d'excellentes relations avec le maître d'hôtel, "Monsieur Paul", un serbe qui parlait bien français, très francophile, et faisait tout pour nous améliorer l'ordinaire du restaurant - Un jour ce M. Paul vint nous trouver et nous expliqua un peu gêné que sa jeune fille de 13 ans était tuberculeuse et que son médecin lui prescrivait du P.A.S., nouveau médicament qu'on ne trouvait alors qu'en Suisse. Il me demanda s'il m'était possible de le lui procurer : je le fis par l'intermédiaire d'un collègue en poste à Genève. Pendant plusieurs jours nous fûmes tenus au courant des effets bénéfiques du médicament.

Il faut ici faire encore une brève digression qui permettra de mieux comprendre la suite. Il était évident que ce "M. Paul", aussi sympathique et serviable qu'il fût, devait, bon gré mal gré, collaborer, étant en contact constant avec tous les étrangers "intéressants" de Belgrade qui constituaient la clientèle de l'hôtel, avec l'UDBA, la police politique yougoslave, alors dirigée par l'amiral Manola.

Quelque temps après, M. Paul vint me trouver à nouveau (ma femme était en France) et m'expliqua, encore plus gêné que la première fois, qu'un de ses bons amis avait lui aussi une fille, amie de la sienne, atteinte elle aussi d'un début de tuberculose et qu'il me serait très reconnaissant si je pouvais faire venir pour elle aussi une dose de PAS, que je lui remis une quinzaine de jours plus tard. Puis, un soir au dîner, M. Paul me dit que son ami tenait à me remercier et m'invitait à aller chez lui le lendemain, vers 22 heures car il travaillait tard. M. Paul m'accompagnerait dans ma voiture pour m'indiquer le chemin. J'acceptai. Le lendemain soir donc, M. Paul me demanda d'aller à Dedinje l'ancien quartier "chic" de Belgrade où étaient installés après la guerre quelques diplomates et beaucoup de gens importante du régime. Je dois marquer une certaine surprise car M. Paul me dit aussitôt que son ami était un homme assez haut placé, me précisant "à toutes fins utiles" et "d'accord avec son ami", que ce dernier, ancien partisan de haut grade était maintenant un collaborateur assez proche de l'amiral Mapola. Il ajouta qu'il n'entrerait pas avec moi car son ami parlait assez bien français et anglais. Du coup cette visite prit un tour d'autant plus intéressant qu'il nous était impossible, à nous occidentaux, d'avoir le moindre contact avec ce genre de personnage.

Je sonnai donc à la porte d'une villa assez belle, entourée d'un jardin qui me parut grand et bien entretenu. Quelle ne fut pas ma surprise quand la porte s'ouvrit et que je vis mon hôte : un magnifique serbe d'une quarantaine d'années, grand, élégamment vêtu, souriant et d'allure distinguée. Il me fit entrer et me présenta sa femme "une ancienne partisane", la copie au féminin de son mari, avec 10 ans de moins et de type plutôt dalmate que serbe. Elle ne parlait que quelques mots d'anglais et son mari servit d'interprète plusieurs fois dans la soirée. Ce qui me frappa aussi d'emblée fut la grande pièce, meublée et décorée assez simplement mais avec goût et ... une grande table tellement chargée de gâteaux, sucreries et bouteilles que je m'attendais à voir arriver de nombreux autres invités, ce qui ne fut pas le cas ! Ils me remercièrent très chaleureusement (elle tenant même à m'embrasser) et lui m'expliqua que leur petite fille unique de 8 ans était née pendant la guerre en 1941 et avait connu pendant ses premières années la vie précaire et pénible des maquis, ce qui expliquait sans doute ce début de tuberculose qui semblait maintenant enrayée... grâce à moi !

J'abrège pour en venir au point qui vous intéresse : après quelques verres

Mon hôte me dit en substance : vous n'ignorez pas quelles sont mes fonctions : elles ne sont pas spécialement faites pour attirer votre sympathie, aussi aimerais-je savoir pour quelles raisons vous nous avez aidés en cette circonstance difficile. Je lui répondis que j'ignorais son métier quand j'avais fait venir le P.A.S mais que cela n'aurait rien changé. Il me semblait suffisant de pouvoir contribuer à guérir une petite fille, quels que soient ses parents. Question et réponse, traduites à sa femme, ~~entraînent~~ entraînent un nouveau verre et un conciliabule avec sa femme. Il me dit alors : j'ai quelque influence dans certains milieux, si vous estimez un jour que je peux vous rendre service, n'hésitez pas à vous adresser à moi (par l'intermédiaire de Pavle). Soudainement le visage de M. Cithon et la promesse que je lui ai faite, vieille d'une quinzaine de jours, me reviennent en mémoire et je me lance à l'eau : vous savez certainement que des ressortissants des pays "kominformistes" (j'emploie le terme abhorré à dessein) voisins de la Yougoslavie sont venus chercher refuge chez vous souvent au péril de leur vie (il fait oui de la tête). Certes ils sont loin d'être tous communistes : ils ont pour beaucoup de la famille en occident, des emplois qui les attendent. Or vous les enfermez dans des camps, hommes, femmes et enfants — Pourquoi ne les laissez-vous pas continuer leur voyage vers les pays qui sont prêts à les accueillir ; vous n'en tireriez que des avantages : vous n'auriez plus à les héberger, à les nourrir, à les surveiller ; votre image à l'occident y gagnerait

Car les camps (de concentration ou similaires) évoquent toujours des souvenirs d'horreur – Quant aux réactions des staliniens elles ne pourraient pas être pires puisqu'ils vous accusent déjà d'être passés aux Américains –

Ces questions n'altérèrent pas la fin de la soirée. Quand je me levai pour partir vers 1 heure du matin, il me dit seulement : « Connaissez-vous un de ces étrangers qui puisse éventuellement servir de cobaye. Je vous promets de réfléchir à la question et de la poser. Je vous tiendrai au courant par téléphone à l'Ambassade. Je lui donnai alors le nom de M. Crihan et celui de son entreprise et je partai non sans qu'ils m'aient encore remercié, dit le regret de ne pas avoir rencontré ma femme dont Pavle leur avait fait une "description dithyrambique", nous avoir souhaité un bon séjour en Yougoslavie malgré les difficultés matérielles compensées un peu par la sympathie des habitants pour les Français, – mais sans m'avoir donné son nom ni son numéro de téléphone – Je ne devais plus les revoir, mais il me téléphona dans les tout premiers jours de juin pour me dire qu'il mettait en route mon "protégé" et que, pour le reste, je serais personnellement contacté par le ministère des Affaires extérieures yougoslaves qui allait recevoir les instructions

L'expérience Crihan se termina bien, encore que dans des conditions un peu rocambolesques (voir le récit qu'il en fait dans sa lettre de Trieste du 26/VI/49). M. Crihan retrouva rapidement sa femme, française, dans la banlieue sud de Paris où elle était professeur. Il fut membre du Comité roumain en exil mais devait mourir peu d'années après.

Pour en revenir à Belgrade, je fus effectivement convoqué dans le courant du mois de juillet au Ministère des Affaires étrangères pour mettre sur pied une procédure permettant le départ des réfugiés. Il fut convenu que l'Ambassade établirait des laissez-passer, revêtus de visas d'entrée en France délivrés par Paris, qui, dotés de visas de sortie de Yougoslavie, seraient remis par les autorités locales aux titulaires en vue de leur départ. Cette procédure, parfois assez lente au début, s'améliora grâce, d'une part à la bienveillance de mon correspondant yougoslave, M. Jakša, conseiller pour les affaires d'Europe occidentale, et du fonctionnaire de la section consulaire chargé de l'apposition des visas de sortie (M. Popović, je crois), d'autre part à la compréhension du Quai d'Orsay qui me laissa rapidement les mains libres, se contentant, pour la forme, d'un télégramme indiquant : "j'ai délivré ce jour un laissez-passer et un visa d'entrée en France à ......, réfugiés roumains ou bulgares etc en Yougoslavie.

Une telle opération ne pouvait se dérouler sans accidents : ceux-ci furent dus, à mon avis, à certaines autorités <u>locales</u> particulièrement lentes à accepter la rupture avec Moscou, comme le prouvent les incidents graves auxquels eut à faire face Tito dans les premières années après cette rupture et les vigoureuses dénonciations des nostalgiques du Kominform dans certaines républiques comme la Macédoine. Deux cas me furent particulièrement pénibles : celui d'un ingénieur roumain qui travaillait dans une grande cimenterie au sud de Belgrade (j'ai oublié son nom), qui

était venu me voir avec sa femme et pour lesquels j'avais établi un laissez-
passer : ils furent reconduits à la frontière roumaine avant d'avoir eu leur
visa de sortie. J'appris par la suite par un de ses collègues serbes qu'il avait
eu le tort, à son retour de l'Ambassade, de se vanter qu'il allait bientôt
partir pour la France, ce qui avait provoqué les réactions de la police de la
petite ville où il résidait.

L'autre est celui de M. et Mme Economu et de leurs deux enfants : ils étaient
venus, eux aussi, me voir à mon bureau. J'avais été séduit par la qualité de
ce couple et par l'étonnante beauté de leurs deux enfants. Mais leur déter-
mination à partir rapidement par n'importe quel moyen m'avait inquiété.
Je leur avais longuement expliqué, en leur citant l'exemple de M. Cruhoa
dont je leur avais fait lire la lettre de Trieste, qu'il était de leur intérêt
de ne prendre aucun risque, de ne pas céder aux provocations de certains
policiers yougoslaves et d'attendre, même au prix de quelques semaines
de captivité supplémentaires, de partir régulièrement. J'eus, quand
ils me quittèrent, l'impression que je ne les avais pas convaincus et
la lettre que je reçus d'eux quelques jours plus tard (copie jointe)
confirma hélas cette impression. C'est dire la peine que je ressentis
en recevant la lettre de mon collègue d'Athènes, Paul Fouchet, qui
m'annonçait que tous les quatre, d'après le rapport de la police frontière
grecque, avaient été abattus, ainsi que quelques autres, par les policiers
yougoslaves. Ceux-ci, après les avoir conduits jusqu'à proximité de la

frontière et leur avoir indiqué le chemin à suivre pour y arriver les auraient mitraillés de dos.

Entièrement différent est le cas du jeune frère Bota ; j'avais reçu avant leur départ pour la France, sa jeune femme Steluta, accompagnée de son beau-frère et de sa belle-sœur. Elle m'avait expliqué que son mari malade (une otite grave, je crois) n'avait pu les accompagner mais les Yougoslaves avaient promis qu'il les suivrait dès sa guérison. Mais elle avait quelque inquiétude car l'U.D.B.A l'avait approché pour lui demander de retourner en Roumanie pour une mission de renseignement. Elle craignait fort que, sa famille partie, les Yougoslaves se fassent plus pressants. Je lui promis de m'occuper de son cas, lui demandant de me donner des nouvelles quelque temps après son arrivée en France ; Ce qu'elle fit par sa lettre du 6 février 1951 (copie jointe) : Son mari n'avait pas donné signe de vie. Pour une fois, je me fâchais auprès de M. Jakša qui n'y était pour rien - J'envisageai même de saisir l'ami de "M. Paul" lorsque je reçus la lettre du 20 mars 1951 par laquelle le jeune Bota m'annonçait son arrivée à Paris.

Voilà donc l'histoire de la naissance de cette "filière" française qui a permis à un certain nombre de "réfugiés" roumains mais aussi à quelques Hongrois, Bulgares et même à un Albanais de gagner l'Occident. J'ajoute que cette "filière" fut jugée si fiable que quatre ambassadeurs (Belgique, Pays-Bas, Italie et même Grande-Bretagne) trouvèrent plus simple de me demander des laissez-passer français pour faire sortir de Yougoslavie des "protégés" auxquels ils tenaient.

The Flatirons, Boulder, Colorado, as viewed beyond the trees in our backyard.

INDEX

D

G

L

M